Basic Instinct

THE UNIVERSITY OF
WINCHESTER

Martial Rose Library
Tel: 01962 827306

SEVEN DAY LOAN ITEM
To be returned on or before the day marked above, subject to recall.

KA 0356375 8

✖ Controversies

Series editors: Stevie Simkin and Julian Petley

Controversies is a series comprising individual studies of controversial films from the late 1960s to the present day, encompassing classic, contemporary Hollywood, cult and world cinema. Each volume provides an in-depth study analysing the various stages of each film's production, distribution, classification and reception, assessing both its impact at the time of its release and its subsequent legacy.

Also published

Shaun Kimber, *Henry: Portrait of a Serial Killer*
Neal King, *The Passion of the Christ*
Stevie Simkin, *Straw Dogs*
Peter Krämer, *A Clockwork Orange*

Forthcoming

Gabrielle Murray, *Bad Boy Bubby*
Jude Davies, *Falling Down*
Julian Petley, *Crash*
Lucy Burke, *The Idiots*
Tim Palmer, *Irreversible*

'The *Controversies* series is a valuable contribution to the ongoing debate about what limits – if any – should be placed on cinema when it comes to the depiction and discussion of extreme subject matter. Sober, balanced and insightful where much debate on these matters has been hysterical, one-sided and unhelpful, these books should help us get a perspective on some of the thorniest films in the history of cinema.'
Kim Newman, novelist, critic and broadcaster

i

Basic Instinct

Stevie Simkin

UNIVERSITY OF WINCHESTER
LIBRARY

© Stevie Simkin 2013

All rights reserved. No reproduction, copy or transmission of this publication may be made without written permission.

No portion of this publication may be reproduced, copied or transmitted save with written permission or in accordance with the provisions of the Copyright, Designs and Patents Act 1988, or under the terms of any licence permitting limited copying issued by the Copyright Licensing Agency, Saffron House, 6–10 Kirby Street, London EC1N 8TS.

Any person who does any unauthorised act in relation to this publication may be liable to criminal prosecution and civil claims for damages.

The author has asserted his right to be identified as the author of this work in accordance with the Copyright, Designs and Patents Act 1988.

First published 2013 by
PALGRAVE MACMILLAN

Palgrave Macmillan in the UK is an imprint of Macmillan Publishers Limited, registered in England, company number 785998, of Houndmills, Basingstoke, Hampshire RG21 6XS.

Palgrave Macmillan in the US is a division of St Martin's Press LLC, 175 Fifth Avenue, New York, NY 10010.

Palgrave Macmillan is the global academic imprint of the above companies and has companies and representatives throughout the world.

Palgrave® and Macmillan® are registered trademarks in the United States, the United Kingdom, Europe and other countries

ISBN: 978–0–230–33692–6

This book is printed on paper suitable for recycling and made from fully managed and sustained forest sources. Logging, pulping and manufacturing processes are expected to conform to the environmental regulations of the country of origin.

A catalogue record for this book is available from the British Library.

A catalog record for this book is available from the Library of Congress.

10	9	8	7	6	5	4	3	2	1
22	21	20	19	18	17	16	15	14	13

Printed in China

UNIVERSITY OF WINCHESTER

For Chuck and Stephie, my two favourite San Franciscans

Contents

Part 1: Making *Basic Instinct*

Part 2: Protesting *Basic Instinct*

Part 3: Censoring *Basic Instinct*

Part 4: Reviewing *Basic Instinct*

Part 5: Reading *Basic Instinct*

Part 6: The Legacy of *Basic Instinct*

Appendices

Acknowledgements

All screen captures taken from *Basic Instinct*, 10th Anniversary Special Edition, Studio Canal/Kinowelt/Momentum Pictures, except Figure 1, taken from *National Lampoon's Loaded Weapon 1*, 1993, 20th Century Fox Entertainment/Pathe/New Line Cinema.

Thanks to the Research and Knowledge Exchange Committee in the Faculty of Arts at the University of Winchester for continued support for my research efforts, including a sabbatical period for early work on this book.

Thanks to our editor at Palgrave Macmillan, Rebecca Barden, for her enthusiasm for the series and her advice on individual volumes.

Thanks to Ed Lamberti at the British Board of Film Classification for securing access to the Board's records on the film for me.

Thanks to my colleagues Dr Helen Grime and Dr Marianne Sharp for valuable dialogue about the film in the early stages of research.

Thanks to my series co-editor Julian Petley for reading the completed manuscript, and for his collaboration on the series as a whole. I continue to learn a great deal from him.

My thanks to my parents, to whom I owe so much.

And finally, thank you to my children, Sophie, Matthew and Jamie, and to my wife, Aileen. I owe you … well, just about everything else.

✕ Introduction

The reasons why what began essentially as a B-movie thriller turned into an important landmark in the history of film controversy in the United States are many and complex. *Basic Instinct*'s notoriety accrued as much through a set of specific circumstances of production and reception as through the content of the film itself. Those circumstances began with the sale of the script, which made headlines in the Hollywood press, and continued as a peculiarly volatile interaction of personality, politics, circumstance and Hollywood hype set the course for the film's troubled production history and reception.

Basic Instinct is also important as an example of a target of so-called grass-roots censorship – in the first instance, the initiative to try and censor it came not from the Motion Picture Association of America (MPAA) or an equivalent censorship body, but from members of the public – in this case, a specific demographic outraged by what they described as homophobia and misogyny in the original screenplay. According to screenwriter Joe Eszterhas, once his script sold for a record-breaking $3 million, 'the whole project was in the middle of a goldfish bowl – it became a very, very public project' (van Scheers, 1997, p. 243). Inevitably, the public nature of the film's very difficult journey to theatrical release and beyond was seized upon by those involved in order to enhance further the status it was to achieve as an 'event movie'.

The fact that *Basic Instinct* had a considerable impact on popular consciousness on its release in 1992 is undeniable. Among other things, the film launched Sharon Stone's career, and, in industry terms, had a profound impact on the profile of the screenwriter in Hollywood (Eszterhas's script prompted a bidding war, and began a cycle of inflated bids for screenplays, raising the status of a number of successful writers in the years that followed).

The film's most infamous scene swiftly established itself as a parody staple: being questioned by police officers, Stone's character Catherine Tramell crosses and uncrosses her legs to reveal, for the benefit of her male interrogators, that she is not wearing any underwear. The 'tributes' started as early as the following year, with an MTV Awards parody by the cast of *The Brady Bunch*. Erotic thriller spoof *Fatal Instinct* (1993) followed, its poster featuring a woman, shot from the shoulders down, seated with her legs crossed, and the legend 'Opening Soon' printed across the image. *Hot Shots! Part Deux* and *Loaded Weapon 1*, in the same year, both included versions of the scene, and there have been scores of references since, on film and on TV, including on popular shows such as *Married with Children* (1992 and 1993), *The Simpsons* (1995), *Seinfeld* (1997), *The X-Files* (2000), *Gilmore Girls* (2002), *My Name Is Earl* (2008) and the UK comedy *Life's Too Short* (2011). In November 2010, Alpine Skier Lindsey Vonn recreated the iconic image of Sharon Stone seated in a tight white dress for the cover of *ESPN – The Magazine*. If imitation is the sincerest form of flattery, Verhoeven, Eszterhas and Stone should feel flattered indeed, although *Loaded Weapon 1*'s smoking beaver might be a stretch (see Figure 1).[1]

This study of *Basic Instinct* attempts to provide a comprehensive account of the film from pre-production, through shooting, post-production and regulation, reception to after-life. The chief focus of the study is, as one would expect, the controversies that it sparked at every stage. Part 1 covers the first stage of the film's history, and considers the production of the film in the context of the industry at the time. Particular attention is paid to the disagreements between screenwriter Joe Eszterhas and director Paul Verhoeven, as well as the shooting of some of the more troublesome scenes, piecing together parts of this process by referring to the accounts of key personnel, including the actors, gleaned from a range of sources.

The second part considers the attempt made by a number of pressure groups, including Queer Nation and the Gay and Lesbian Alliance Against Defamation (GLAAD), to persuade the director, writer and production team to make changes to take account of their objections to what they perceived as a

Figure 1: From *Loaded Weapon 1*'s parody of the interrogation scene.

homophobic and misogynist screenplay. When this effort failed, the groups switched strategy and did all they could to disrupt the location shooting of the movie. The discussion gives due consideration to those on both sides of the divide (and those that crossed from one side to the other, notably Eszterhas himself), and takes account of the reflections of actors, writer and director, in some cases with the benefit of hindsight. In order to judge the protests against the film fairly, it is important to understand the wider context of representations of homosexuality and bisexuality in Hollywood, and in US society more generally at this time. My overview considers in particular William Friedkin's cop thriller *Cruising* (1980), which, with its controversial depiction of the gay and S&M scene in New York City, stirred similar trouble ten years before *Basic Instinct*. Part 2 attempts to make sense of some of the associated issues, including the heated debate about freedom of speech and political correctness, while also offering an assessment of the charges of homophobia and misogyny levelled against *Basic Instinct*.

Part 3 begins with an overview of the state of film censorship in the US at the time *Basic Instinct* was made. The MPAA and Classification and Rating Administration (CARA) were attempting at this time to launch a new adult rating of NC-17 to replace the X certificate, which had long since been rejected by the major studios and appropriated instead by the porn industry. The conflicting interests that came into play at this point – artistic, commercial, regulatory – are complex and worth untangling. The second section of Part 3 looks very closely and precisely at the footage cut at the request of the MPAA (the film was released uncut in the UK and in most other countries, but had to shed around forty seconds for the domestic audience). The intact scenes are compared with their R-rated edited versions and the implications of the cuts are analysed. The third section considers the deliberations of the British Board of Film Classification (BBFC). Although it was passed uncut at 18 in the UK, the examiners' reports are interesting for what they reveal about the Board's attitudes towards sex, violence and sexual violence at this time.[2] There is also some discussion of letters written to the Board by members of the public objecting to its decision to certificate the film in its uncut form.

Part 4 considers the reception of the film. There is an extensive survey of the US press reaction, as well as the critical response in the UK, but I also discuss in detail the strategies the pressure groups adopted in this third stage of their campaign against the film. Having attempted to enforce changes to the script and then to disrupt the shoot, they proceeded to make concerted efforts to spoil the film's opening weekend, sparking fresh debates about the limits of protest and where it begins to impinge on freedom of expression. Part 5 provides the most extensive critical discussion of the film and its contested meanings. *Basic Instinct* is considered in the context of a wave of films featuring violent women, and is also placed in the context of the genre to which it owes most, *film noir*. I examine the complex power relations between men and women that the film maps out, including a close analysis of the interrogation scene: when Catherine appears to be at her most 'exposed', she is least vulnerable. The paradoxical cross-currents of gender and power are evaluated and then related back to the debates over the film's misogyny and homophobia. Finally, Part 6 tries to assess the status of the film's politics of gender and sexuality twenty years on. The conclusion also raises questions about the nature of representation, and the relation between representation and the 'real', partly via a reading of the press coverage of a notorious murder case from 2007 featuring a woman portrayed by some elements of the media as a 'real life' *femme fatale*.

Basic Instinct was undoubtedly a ground-breaking movie, particularly for the way it redrew the boundaries of the depiction of (relatively) graphic sex in mainstream film. It also raises important questions about the politics of representation with regard to gender and sexuality. Furthermore, few popular movies of its era have attracted such a degree of attention from academics in the fields of film and cultural studies. Indeed, it is at the intersection of the popular and the scholarly that *Basic Instinct* is perhaps most provocative. The book attempts to keep both in focus throughout, and concludes with some reflections on the film's legacy in terms of shifts in ideologies of gender and violence, and the way these might filter through popular culture into popular consciousness.

✕ Synopsis

The film opens with a sex scene in which a blonde woman, her face never clearly visible to the audience, straddles her male lover, ties his hands to the bed with a white silk scarf, and stabs him to death with an ice-pick. While she continues her frenzied attack, we cut abruptly to an establishing shot of the street, with a cop car arriving outside the murder scene. The car's occupants join a forensic team examining the bedroom and the body of the murder victim: Johnny Boz (Bill Cable) was a retired rock star and a friend of the San Francisco Mayor. The two detectives from the car, Nick Curran (Michael Douglas) and Gus Moran (George Dzundza), are despatched to question Boz's lover Catherine Tramell (Sharon Stone). At Tramell's opulent home, they find only her lesbian lover Roxy (Leilani Sarelle), who directs them to Tramell's beach-house. There, when questioned about the murder, Tramell gives nothing away, and is apparently unmoved by news of Boz's death.

At the station, the audience is introduced to police psychologist Beth Garner (Jeanne Tripplehorn) and two things become clear: Nick has been under psychological evaluation, and Nick and Beth have until recently been in a relationship. At a briefing, Nick and Gus hear that Catherine Tramell, a millionaire with a degree in psychology and a successful author of detective fiction, has written a book about the murder of a retired rock star. Beth and her colleague Dr Lamott (Stephen Tobolowsky) provide the investigating team with a psychological profile of Tramell, and Nick and Gus are sent to bring her in for formal questioning. During the interrogation, she unnerves the detectives by speaking openly of her enjoyment of sex and drugs. At one point, she uncrosses and recrosses her legs, revealing to the police interrogators that she is naked beneath her skirt. She passes a lie-detector test, and is released without charge. Nick, who seems convinced of her guilt regardless, drives her home.

Nick, who has been teetotal since disciplinary action was brought against him after an accidental shooting, joins his fellow cops at a bar and orders a whisky. Taunted by Internal Affairs investigator Nilsen (Daniel von Bargen), Nick almost comes to blows with him, and leaves with Beth. They go to her apartment, where their sexual encounter is pitched somewhere between aggressive sex and an act of rape.

Nick hears more of Catherine's background, which includes a number of traumatic bereavements: we have already heard of the deaths of her parents in a boating accident when she was a teenager, and of a former lover, boxing champion Manny Vasquez. Now Nick is informed that one of her professors was stabbed to death with an ice-pick during her college days at Berkeley. Nick stakes out Catherine's home and follows her in his car when she leaves. Aware she is being followed, she leads him on a dangerous chase down hilltop roads. Left trailing, he eventually spots her car parked outside the house of a woman named Hazel Dobkins (Dorothy Malone). When he tries to tail her home, she again loses him in traffic. Nick arrives back at her house and watches from her garden as she undresses at the window. Returning to the station to find out more about Dobkins, he meets Gus, who tells him that many years ago Hazel Dobkins was convicted of the murders of her husband and three children.

Nick visits Catherine at her beachfront house, where he learns that she has accessed confidential information about him, and that she is using him as the basis for the main character in her next novel. It becomes increasingly obvious that there is sexual tension between the two of them, but the scene ends with Catherine embracing and fondling Roxy as Nick turns and leaves. Nick returns to the station and challenges Beth, who admits that she passed his file to Nilsen. Curran confronts the IA officer and has to be restrained. That night, Nick is at home alone drinking when Beth appears. They argue and fight when Nick takes back the key to his apartment and dismisses their relationship as worthless. Beth tells Nick she had to give Nilsen his file to save him from being fired from the force. Later the same night, Nilsen is found dead in his car, shot in the head, and Nick is inevitably a suspect. In a scene that mirrors Catherine's interrogation, Nick is questioned, but Beth comes to his aid with an alibi, claiming that Nick was not drunk when she left his apartment, but sober and lucid.

Nick is no longer considered a suspect but is forced to go on leave pending a psychiatric evaluation. He returns home to find Catherine waiting outside. After another cat-and-mouse exchange, she tells him she will be at Johnny Boz's club that night and he says he will meet her there, which is where the following scene is set. Catherine and Nick dance, and then leave for her beachfront house. They have sex, during which Catherine ties Nick to the bed with a white silk scarf. Afterwards, while Catherine sleeps, Nick goes to the bathroom, and Roxy appears. She tells him that Catherine likes her to watch while she has sex with men. The next morning, Nick talks with Catherine, pronouncing their love-making 'the fuck of the century'. Catherine is cool and mildly amused by Nick's enthusiasm. Nick admits he is in love with Catherine but insists he will still 'nail her' for the murder of Johnny Boz.

That evening, Nick finds a drunk Gus in a club, and Gus is angry when he figures out what has happened between Nick and Catherine. Just after Gus leaves the parking lot, Nick is almost run down by a car. Nick gives chase in his own vehicle and a game of chicken results in the other car careering off a bridge. When Nick surveys the wreckage, he finds the driver dead: Roxy. The next day, he is invited to the station for his psychological evaluation; he mocks the psychiatric team and leaves for Catherine's beachfront house, where he finds her mourning Roxy. They make love. Afterwards, Catherine mentions a woman who was obsessed with her at college. Back at the station, Nick and Gus learn that Roxy also had a violent past, having killed her two brothers with a razor when she was sixteen years old. Nick visits the Berkeley campus to check Catherine's story about the woman from her college days but draws a blank. When he challenges her about it, and she corrects the name, he finds the driving licence in the woman's record, and it turns out to be Beth. Beth admits that she knew Catherine, but claims it was Tramell who was obsessed with her. She explains her name change by revealing she was briefly married to a doctor in Salinas.

Catherine denies Beth's version and reveals she filed a report on Beth at the time. When Nick tries to check this out, it turns out that Nilsen has already pulled the file; this has left Nick convinced that Beth is the murderer, despite Gus's attempt to get him to see sense. Nick returns home to find Catherine waiting, and they make love. The next day, he visits the clinic where Beth's former husband worked and discovers the doctor was shot dead five or six years earlier, and no-one was ever convicted, although there had been talk of the wife having had a female lover. It also turns out that Nilsen had recently visited asking similar questions.

Nick returns to Catherine's house, now even more convinced of Beth's guilt. Catherine has finished her book and is cold and dismissive towards him. A short time later, Gus finds Nick and tells him he has traced Tramell's room-mate from college and has arranged to meet her at a hotel. They drive there together and Gus persuades Nick to remain in the car. A few moments later, Nick suddenly realises that Gus is walking into a trap. He runs into the hotel and up the stairs, but Gus has already been brutally stabbed in the neck multiple times, and he dies in the elevator as Nick kneels beside him. Nick emerges from the elevator to find himself face to face with Beth. Convinced she is the killer, Nick trains a gun on her and tells her to take her hands out of her pockets. As she does, Nick believes he spies a gun in her hand, and shoots her down, only to find that she has nothing in her pockets beside an over-sized keyring we saw in an earlier scene. However, evidence found in the stairwell – an ice-pick, a blonde wig, a police-department jacket – and further evidence found in Beth's flat (including the gun that killed Nilsen) convinces the authorities that Beth was the killer.

Nick returns home to find Catherine, who says, having lost everyone close to her, she has decided she doesn't want to lose him. They make love, and when Catherine asks him what happens next, he says they will 'fuck like minks

… and live happily ever after'. As they lie in bed and Nick smokes, Catherine turns away from him and stretches an arm down towards the floor. Then they embrace and kiss again. The camera fades out and back in as they continue to kiss. Finally, as the camera pans down to the floor, an ice-pick is revealed, lying just underneath the bed.

✖ PART 1

MAKING *BASIC INSTINCT*

From *Love Hurts* to *Basic Instinct*: Joe Eszterhas

The story of *Basic Instinct*'s production history is a peculiarly Hollywood-style tale of hype, million-dollar deals and strong personalities, among which the screenwriter Joe Eszterhas is probably the most remarkable. Born in Hungary in 1944, his family moved to the United States in 1950 and settled in Cleveland, Ohio. Eszterhas's career began in journalism, working in the early 1970s for the *Cleveland Plain Dealer* and then writing for *Rolling Stone* magazine in San Francisco. When *Rolling Stone* shifted its base to New York City, Eszterhas was reluctant to move, and it was at this point, casting around for a career change that would allow him to remain in the Bay Area, that he began work on his first screenplay. *F.I.S.T* (1978) was a drama about the truckers' union movement set in the 1930s. The director, Norman Jewison, acted as the writer's mentor through the protracted genesis of the script, and the project ended up under the blessing and the curse of the casting of Sylvester Stallone in a lead role. Stallone had recently established himself as a major star via the runaway success of *Rocky* (1976), and *F.I.S.T.* consequently attracted more attention among critics and audiences than it might have done otherwise; at the same time, some of the dramatic focus of the movie was probably lost in the blaze of Stallone's star billing. It was several years before Eszterhas's next project got off the desk and into production, but *Flashdance* (1983), directed by Adrian Lyne, though initially a critical and commercial failure, developed via word of mouth into a massive hit, eventually grossing over $400 million worldwide.

Eszterhas was now establishing himself as a major player in his own right. Genre-hopping once again, he scripted the sensationalistic courtroom dramatic thriller *Jagged Edge* (1985). Originally intended as a project for Jane Fonda, the actress was dropped from the project when she expressed dissatisfaction with the draft, demanding rewrites, according to Eszterhas himself (2005, pp. 186–7). Under Richard Marquand's direction, the movie went ahead with Glenn Close in the Fonda role of the lawyer and Jeff Bridges as the man accused of the savage murder of his wife. The film was another word-of-mouth hit. Less successful credits followed – the appalling Bob Dylan vehicle *Hearts of Fire* (1987), and two thrillers, *Betrayed* (1988) and *Music Box* (1989), both directed by Costa-Gavras, and neither attracting significant audiences. Casting around for inspiration again, Eszterhas chose to exercise a growing interest in *film noir* by writing, apparently at breakneck pace, the first draft of 'a thriller with a strong sexual content' that he christened *Love Hurts* (Eszterhas, 2005, p. 268).[3] Just before sending it to his agent, Guy McElwaine, he re-opened the envelope and typed up a new cover sheet, renaming it *Basic Instinct*.

It was now June 1990. Eszterhas, fresh from an acrimonious split with the Hollywood agency CAA headed by Hollywood power-player Mike Ovitz, was on the open market; the *Basic Instinct* script was, in effect, put up for auction. This was a relatively recent trend in the business: it was much more common for studios to buy 'treatments' – story outlines – which would then be developed, often by a team of writers, under the close supervision of studio executives (McNary, 1990, p. C6). But Eszterhas would become one of the leading figures in a decisive industry shift which the editor of *Show Biz News* described as an 'increased emphasis on concepts and material, rather than on stars and directors' (Alex Ben Block cited in McNary, 1990, p. C6). The bidding war took less than twenty-four hours to complete, with Disney, Universal, Warner Brothers, Tri-Star, Columbia and Paramount, as well as the independents Carolco, Cinergi and Imagine all involved (*Variety*, 1990, p. 10). The key contenders were two former associates: Cinergi was headed by Andrew Vajna, who had recently been bought out of his partnership in Carolco by the company's co-founder Mario Kassar. Kassar and Vajna were bitter competitors, each intent on scoring the latest, hottest item on the Hollywood scene, and it was this intense rivalry that fuelled the bidding war: Kassar paid a reported $3 million to the writer plus a further million to Irvin

Winkler to produce. Eszterhas would also receive gross points on the movie's takings once the company had broken even on its investment (*Variety*, 1990, p. 10). The signing shattered the previous record payout of $1.75 million for Shane Black's *The Last Boy Scout* (1991) which had already taken the industry by surprise. Black had secured the deal only a couple of months earlier, in April 1990, after the success of *Lethal Weapon* (1987), which he had written, and its sequel (1989), for which he had provided the story.

However, even while Eszterhas celebrated, trouble was brewing. In October 1990, without consulting Winkler, Carolco signed Michael Douglas for the lead role of Nick Curran (for another record sum of $15 million) and, although Eszterhas and Winkler were happy enough with the result of the casting choice, the fact that the decision had been made without consulting them seemed ominous. It was only a foretaste of what was to come. Next, Kassar insisted on nominating the director for the project. Eszterhas and Winkler wanted Milos Forman, but, having tried and failed to secure Adrian Lyne's signature, Kassar instead chose Paul Verhoeven – a Dutch director who had scored two notable Hollywood science-fiction hits with *RoboCop* (1987) and *Total Recall* (1990). Kassar and Andrew Vajna had been executive producers on the latter, an Arnold Schwarzenegger vehicle based on a Philip K. Dick short story. Kassar, a European, also knew Verhoeven's Dutch films, including *The Fourth Man* (1984), a film Verhoeven has repeatedly described as, in metaphorical terms, a *Basic Instinct* prequel.[4]

An early meeting between Eszterhas and Verhoeven left the writer feeling increasingly uncomfortable: Verhoeven's background in realism and his track record of including graphic nudity in his Dutch-made films were well known. Now he made it clear that he would be shooting the sex scenes in *Basic Instinct* with a correspondingly high degree of candour. Furthermore, in one notable interview around the same time, Verhoeven had already indicated his intention to direct the first mainstream film to include a shot of an erect penis. Eszterhas was unimpressed. 'I viewed my script as a psychosexual thriller with erotic content but I didn't want it to turn into porn,' he wrote, reflecting back on his experience.

UNIVERSITY OF WINCHESTER
LIBRARY

> All the scenes in the script with any nudity had a descriptive tag line:
> *'It is dark. We can't see clearly'.* Irwin and I wanted those scenes to be
> about shadows and arty camera angles, not about skin, and certainly
> not about full-frontal nudity. (Eszterhas, 2005, p. 293)

Verhoeven objected, not unreasonably, that one could not shoot love scenes
entirely in the dark, and remained insistent that the nudity would be graphic
and visible (McGregor, 1992, p. 19).

According to Eszterhas, neither Douglas nor Verhoeven liked his
script. Douglas had the status of key leading man in Hollywood at the time
thanks to his pedigree and in particular his recent successes with the adventure
movies *Romancing the Stone* (1984) and *The Jewel of the Nile* (1985). The
success of the erotic thriller *Fatal Attraction* (1987), adding an edgier, more
ambivalent quality to his profile, probably gave him an advantage over some
of his contenders for the role of Nick Curran; other candidates had included
Richard Gere, Mel Gibson and Kevin Costner. He had also been able to
negotiate a say in both script and casting into his contract. At a meeting
between star, director and writer, Verhoeven repeatedly asked Eszterhas what
the screenplay was about, and when the writer tried to explain that it was
'about evil and psychological and sexual manipulation and homicidal impulse,'
the director, Eszterhas claims, 'looked at me blankly'. Douglas, meanwhile,
was preoccupied with the downbeat ending ('Where is the redemption here?',
he demanded), and fretted that Catherine Tramell consistently had the upper
hand over his own character: in an interview conducted at the time the film
premiered, he described his character in the original script as 'too passive' ...
'He [Nick] was always being a device unto *her* [emphasis in the original] ...
Catherine Tramell delegated all the moves' (Rohrer, 1992). When Verhoeven
insisted on changes, Eszterhas dug in his heels, and the two were soon
shouting across the table at each other, with Verhoeven assuming the
conventional director-as-*auteur* dominant position.

The conflict is one that would come to define Eszterhas's career.
Eszterhas's account of the meeting crystallises it neatly in Verhoeven's

reported phrase, 'Look, I am the director, *ja*? And you are the writer. So I am right and you are wrong, *ja*?' (cited in van Scheers, 1997, p. 294). For Eszterhas, this distinction defined precisely the reason why Verhoeven had no right to demand script changes: the script was his, and, as far as he was concerned, Verhoeven should stick to what he did best: directing. At the same time, Eszterhas was very acutely aware that his insistence on maintaining the integrity of his script was not in line with customary Hollywood industry practice. Meanwhile, with his fears about Verhoeven's plans confirmed, after a good deal of agonising over the right course of action, and in consultation with his agent McElwaine, Eszterhas first of all tried and failed to buy the script back off Carolco. At that point, he told Adrian Silbey, 'The only choice I then had was to go along with something I felt would violate my own artistic and creative standards or withdraw' (cited in Silbey, 1990, p. 25). His friend Irwin Winkler backed him up by walking away too, complaining publicly that he had been 'mugged' into accepting Verhoeven who, he felt, was 'obsessed with showing people's bodies "in various states of excitement"' (Rohrer, 1992). In his own press statement, Eszterhas claimed 'philosophical and personal differences' with the director and mentioned both of his key objections: Verhoeven's aim to shoot a 'sexually explicit thriller' and the difference of opinion over how the relationship between writer and director should work (Eszterhas, 2005, pp. 295–6). According to Verhoeven, the director went on holiday after his first meeting with Winkler and Eszterhas, and fully expected to return for a further round of talks. However, by the time he came back, Winkler and Eszterhas had already walked, ensuring that the news made the headlines in the Hollywood daily, *Variety*. Exasperated by Verhoeven's priorities, which, they felt, de-emphasised the mystery thriller aspect of the project to focus primarily on eroticism, they not only washed their hands of it but made sure that the washing was as public and ritualistic as possible.

Beginning around December 1990, Verhoeven worked hard on the *Basic Instinct* script with Gary Goldman, who had done some successful polishing on the *Total Recall* project. The two of them attempted to work a love scene between Catherine Tramell and Roxy into the storyline, and made the sex scenes between Catherine and Nick more detailed and explicit. Both Goldman and Verhoeven felt that the story needed to expand on the Roxy/Catherine relationship, and that Eszterhas had chosen not to write the scene out of a sense of 'delicacy' (Goldman cited in van Scheers, 1997, p. 245). They tried to insert the Roxy/Catherine love scene at the point where Curran finds out that a copy of his personal file has been given to Catherine. Verhoeven intention's was that, as Nick left to confront Beth, the camera would linger with the two women, who would kiss and begin to make love, 'as if to say,' Verhoeven explains, '"We don't need you, Nick, we've got each other"' (van Scheers, 1997, p. 245). However, the insertion of a love scene between the women at this point, Verhoeven and Goldman discovered, only served to hold up the narrative at a crucial stage, and the plotting suffered significantly as a result (McGregor, 1992, p. 20). Fortunately, narrative tension won out over titillation, and the scene was dropped.

Casting Catherine

In the meantime, the casting of the role of Catherine was becoming a significant problem. According to various reports, candidates included almost every eligible female star of the era: Debra Winger, Ellen Barkin, Demi Moore, Geena Davis (a favourite candidate of Verhoeven's, Davis was apparently unimpressed with the script's gender politics), Emma Thompson, Kelly Lynch, Kim Basinger, Julia Roberts, Melanie Griffith, Greta Scacchi, Isabelle Adjani (Douglas's choice), Lena Olin and Michelle Pfeiffer, who was reportedly 'disgusted' by the sex scenes (Bouzereau, 1994, p. 181; Keesey and Duncan, 2005, p. 126; Johnson and Dwyer, 1992; *Daily Mail*, 1991). In fact it would seem that most, if not all of them, were put off by Verhoeven's plans to push the boundaries of the mainstream depiction of sex on screen. The division between the Hollywood women's A-list (where non-nudity contracts could usually be negotiated fairly easily by actresses' agents) and the B-list (where nudity was often a requirement in genres such as R-rated thrillers) was very marked. There were a couple of exceptions: Kelly McGillis and Mariel Hemingway, according to Eszterhas's memoir, were keen and unperturbed by the sex scenes, but both screentested poorly (2005, p. 296). The search for Catherine Tramell continued. In the meantime, reports mentioned that Anne Archer was being considered for the part of Beth (*Daily Mail*, 1991, p. 23), although the role would eventually go to Jeanne Tripplehorn, in her début feature-film performance.

By February 1991, having spent some considerable time on rewrites, Verhoeven concluded that the script required no substantial changes after all. Eszterhas claims that what Verhoeven sent him, in a bid at reconciliation, was '*my* first draft, *word for word, scene for scene*' [Eszterhas's italics] (2005, p. 297). Other reports suggest there may have been a dozen or so minor line changes. Whatever the precise details may be, it seems clear that the 'new' screenplay was almost entirely Eszterhas's own work and in late February or early March 1991, a reunion between Eszterhas and Verhoeven was sealed over dinner (McGregor, 1992, p. 20): in keeping with the pattern that had been established of taking every opportunity to keep the project in the gossip columns, the détente was staged at 'a very public prime-table dinner at Morton's' (Eszterhas, 2005, p. 297). Eszterhas was impressed with the Dutchman's willingness to admit he had made a mistake, and to admit it publicly: Verhoeven welcomed him back to the project in a meeting with the *Daily Variety* newspaper the next morning (p. 297). However, despite the writer's protestations, Winkler did not return, since Alan Marshall was now firmly settled in the producer's role.

The conflict between Eszterhas and Verhoeven, and its very public display, was significant in terms of the way power games would play out in Hollywood in the future. Regardless of the quality of his screenplays, Eszterhas's historical significance as a screenwriter in the context of the business side of Hollywood is now undeniable. Eszterhas quotes the *Denver Post*'s description of him as 'the screenwriter as rock star' (2007, p. 103), a neat assessment of the kind of status he acquired around this time, in large part as a result of the newsworthy battles over his screenplay for *Basic Instinct*. His memoir *Hollywood Animal* is fired by a sense of indignation and fierce pride in his craft and an unshakable belief in the importance (and traditionally grossly undervalued status) of the screenwriter in Hollywood. Impatient with the tendency to *auteur*-ise the director, Eszterhas insisted on the primacy of the writer who, in his estimation, should be understood as the composer, with the director as the conductor, and the actors and crew 'part of the orchestra' (2005, p. 34). The script was 'my creation', he argued, and the film-making process itself a separate act, a collaboration between director, actors and crew. The fact that Verhoeven finally had to admit defeat and return to the writer's original draft, he believes, proved his point: 'I saved my script from being destroyed by my intransigence and my willingness to fight' (Eszterhas, 2007, p. 215). In an industry preoccupied with the ordering of names and roles in the film's opening credits, Eszterhas's achievement of having his screenwriting credit at the beginning of *Showgirls* (1995) *after* the producers' and just before the director's was a major coup, and a testament to his change in status.

Meanwhile, another potential Catherine Tramell had appeared on the horizon. Thirty-two-year-old Sharon Stone, who had played the part of Schwarzenegger's duplicitous wife in *Total Recall*, had been brought in to do some looping for an edited, in-flight movie version of the Schwarzenegger film. According to the press release for the film, Stone was determined to take advantage of the opportunity to put herself in the frame for *Basic Instinct* and came dressed as Catherine Tramell. 'I did the whole number', she confessed: 'Cocktail dress, French twist, etc. I told Paul I was going to a cocktail party. I was afraid to ask him to test me so I wanted to demonstrate to him that I understood how to be like her.'[5] Stone had spent over a decade scrabbling up the B-list, graduating from television shows such as *Magnum P.I.* (1980–8) and *Bay City Blues* (1983) to cheap and schlocky movies with titles such as *The Calendar Girl Murders* (1984) and *Cold Steel* (1987), low-grade action movies including *Action Jackson* and *Above the Law* (both 1988), and poor people's Indiana Jones clones such as *King Solomon's Mines* (1985) and *Allan Quatermain and the Lost City of Gold* (1986). However, in 1990, her casting in Verhoeven's *Total Recall*, and her performance in that film – in particular, her ability to switch from loving and attentive wife to cold killer – had evidently made a strong impression on the director. Since *Total Recall*, she had made three more films, but none of them had been noteworthy. In fact, her most astute career move in the preceding couple of years had probably been agreeing to appear nude for *Playboy* magazine in 1990, something that raised her profile more successfully than any of her film roles during that period. According to her post-*Basic Instinct Playboy* interview (December 1992), she had had the script for the film for some time, but had declined to read it, convinced that she would not be in the running for such a high-profile film. The issue of a balance between male and female lead in terms of experienced star power remained problematic: Michael Douglas apparently dismissed the suggestion that Stone should play opposite him on account of her lack of experience and of star status: '"I thought, all right, I'll handle this, but I want somebody of equal stature to share the risks"', is how he put it in an interview with *Entertainment Weekly* after the film had premiered (Rohrer, 1992).

Both Verhoeven and the Carolco executives, however, were impressed with Stone's screentest. Tape of the test is available on DVD, and it is clear why she made a strong impression:[6] her portrayal is rather warmer and more gently playful than the character she would create for the film, but the striking combination of watchful intelligence, self-possession and seductiveness is already in place. 'She was Catherine Tramell from the moment she started to talk,' according to Verhoeven (Bouineau, 2001, p. 43). After Stone tested, the search continued for several months. 'Nobody wanted Sharon because she was unknown, but I wanted her because I knew her from *Total Recall* and I thought that she could do it,' Verhoeven said (Bouineau, 2001, p. 43). The director eventually persuaded Douglas to try some scenes with her, and the tests finally convinced his star actor. Stone was signed for $300,000, a fee dwarfed by Verhoeven's take ($5 million), and a small fraction of Douglas's ($15 million), but, for her, it would prove to be that elusive step up into mainstream Hollywood stardom. Even then, Stone almost threw away the opportunity on the first day of shooting, suffering a catastrophic crisis of confidence. In their DVD commentary, cinematographer Jan de Bont and the director discuss the episode while Stone's first on-screen appearance plays; they recall her nervousness, and how wooden her performance was as a result; apparently, there was even talk, in the wake of the disastrous first day, of replacing her. Verhoeven had to stop filming and take her aside to give her a pep talk, convincing her that she could pull this performance off (Keesey and Duncan, 2005, p. 127). The following day, Stone reappeared on set transformed, and from that point on, so the story goes, she did not look back.

'What Exactly Did You Have in Mind?' Shooting the Sex Scenes

I have already discussed the early controversy over the sex scenes in the film: Eszterhas had envisaged the scenes as dimly lit, filmed in an oblique, art-house style. Verhoeven's intentions were very different, and from the earliest stages, *Basic Instinct* was promoted as a movie that was going to shatter the boundaries of mainstream Hollywood film in terms of its sexual content. Of course, films involving nudity always present a number of difficulties. The hurdles begin at the casting stage, with Verhoeven's forthrightness about what he would require of his female lead. When actors have been selected, the Screen Actors Guild requires nudity waivers to be signed as part of the contract between actor and producers, and such waivers have to be very specific about what is permissible and what is not: Douglas was clear that he would not allow his genitals to be shown on screen (a brief glimpse in long shot and profile is visible in the uncut version of the film, but seems to have been digitally masked in the US cut). There is, however, an instance of full-frontal male nudity in the movie, one that Verhoeven asked his producer Alan Marshall to clear with the MPAA before submission: at the crime scene after the film's opening sequence, Johnny Boz's corpse is seen naked, lying on the bed; 'the MPAA's comment was that as long as it's dead meat, it's fine', Verhoeven told Laurent Bouzereau; 'They didn't phrase it that way, but that's basically the idea' (1994, p. 202) (see Figure 2). Since the actor playing Boz

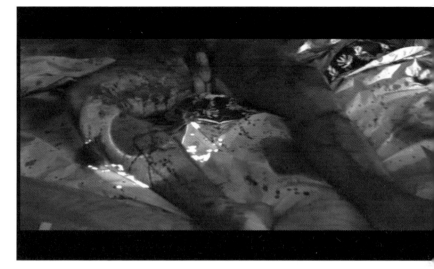

Figure 2: 'Dead Meat'.

had to do little apart from have sex, look orgasmic, and then scream as he was stabbed to death, they chose to recruit someone from the porn industry (Bill Cable) to play the role.

It should come as no surprise, perhaps, that the same rules do not apply to Hollywood actresses. During the prolonged casting process for *Basic Instinct*, the issue of (female) nudity evidently scared away a number of A-list Hollywood stars who otherwise might have jumped at the chance of taking on a role that was bound to make an impression – a striking characterisation, a role that dominates the film, playing opposite one of Hollywood's most powerful figures, in a movie that promised to be one of the key mainstream releases of the year. It is perhaps indicative of Stone's interstitial status at the time that she grabbed the opportunity with both hands and refused to let go. As Linda Ruth Williams points out, 'Willingness to meet the nudity requirement has [...] been viewed as one of the essential differences between A- and B-list performers'. Williams singles out Stone as an example of an A-lister (which she certainly was post-*Basic Instinct*) who starts with nude roles 'and then spends the rest of their career trying to escape them' (Williams, 2005, p. 302). Stone's next role after *Basic Instinct* certainly suggested this might set the pace for her career on the A-list: *Sliver* (1993) was sold almost exclusively on a one-two punch of sexual content and Stone's newly established star power. The film was a disappointment, however, trashed by critics and largely ignored by audiences: although it took $12 million in its opening weekend (compared to *Basic Instinct*'s $15 million), its total US gross was only $36.3 million (compared to almost $118 million). Stone's approach to her character, Carly Norris, found her exchanging danger and power for vulnerability, but it was hardly an impressive career move. Following this misstep, Stone's next roles found her shifting away from sex-symbol status to more serious parts, first as the wronged wife in *Intersection* (1994) and then, following a co-star billing with Sylvester Stallone for *The Specialist* (1994) and Sam Raimi's offbeat Western *The Quick and the Dead* (1995), more heavyweight acting (and no nudity) in the company of Martin Scorsese and Robert De Niro for *Casino* (1995).

According to her own reflections and anecdotes, once filming of *Basic Instinct* began, Stone seemed to come to terms with the requirement for extensive nudity at an early stage. In her *Playboy* interview publicising the film, she recalls shooting the key sex scene with Douglas in an amusing anecdote:

> … we were getting ready to do a take, and Michael put his cappuccino down on the side of the bed – not the camera side. At the last second I took off my robe, tossed it over the side of the bed and heard the cappuccino fall over onto the white carpeting. Forgetting the fact that, at that moment, I was supposed to be behaving like a movie star and not like some middle-class girl from Pennsylvania, I leapt over the side of the bed, screaming, 'Oh, my God!' Only then did I realize that everybody in the room now knows me better than my gynaecologist does. … But you know what? We've all got the same stuff. I don't know what the big deal is, really. (Sheff, 1992)

It is likely, too, that the process of applying full body make-up for the sex scenes would have had a psychological effect. Make-up artist David Craig Forrest describes it as 'a sort of second skin, so people aren't seeing the "raw" you', while the process of applying it also helps the actors adjust to being seen naked, and to being touched (Garey, 1992, p. 50). Pushed a little further to admit whether or not she found the nudity and sex scenes 'scary', Stone responded with the kind of cutting riposte that she became famous for in her interviews around this time: 'I am infinitely less comfortable with the fact that the public is more concerned with whether or not I was nude or gay than whether or not I was a fucking serial killer. Excuse me very much, but where are your priorities, people?' (Sheff, 1992).

If Sharon Stone managed to reconcile herself to the nudity required by the sex scenes she had to shoot, the filming of the interrogation scene and the infamous crotch shot was not as easily dismissed. The debate over who first proposed the idea of Catherine flashing her genitalia during the interrogation scene has been ongoing ever since Stone claimed in interviews publicising the movie that Verhoeven misled her on set about exactly what would be visible in the final cut. Although this particular scene was not problematic for either the MPAA or for the protesters trying to disrupt the shoot, it was the scene that would finally be responsible for the movie's enduring reputation. As I noted in the introduction, the leg-crossing scene has been imitated and parodied in many films and TV shows, as well as homemade online videos available via sites such as YouTube, since *Basic Instinct* was first released. It was even awarded the dubious honour of being the most paused scene in the history of British television (Metro.co.uk, 2011). The scene has rightly been identified as the film's key moment in popular critical as well as academic analysis, and full discussion of different perspectives on it can be found in Part 5 (see pp. 113–18). Like many such scenes, however, the precise details of how it came to be filmed the way it did remain obscured by contradictory versions from the different people involved.

According to a number of accounts (see, for example, van Scheers, 1997, pp. 233–4), the original inspiration was buried in Verhoeven's memory: as a twenty-year-old at a student party in Holland, he remembered watching as a friend sat chatting, periodically crossing and uncrossing her legs. According to the anecdote, Verhoeven's friend Robert Haverschmidt asked her if she knew that they could 'see everything'. 'Of course,' she said. 'That's why I'm doing it.' However, at least for a while, in particular during early publicity junkets for the movie, Stone asserted that discarding her underwear for the scene had been *her* idea. Within months, she would change her story and claim that Verhoeven had tricked her: according to Stone, Verhoeven had promised to make sure the scene was so dimly lit that nothing would be visible. She claimed to have been so shocked when she first saw the finished scene that she marched into the projecting room and slapped the director across the face. In the December 1992 *Playboy* interview, she refused to discuss the incident ('water under the bridge'), but Munn's biography, which is apparently based on a couple of long interviews with Stone herself, gives an extensive take on her side of the story. She claims Verhoeven asked her to remove her panties because they were reflecting light back at the camera. She said he had promised her that her nakedness would be obscured by discreet lighting, and that when she first saw the finished version of the scene, in a private screening at Carolco, among an audience that included many strangers as well as friends and associates of hers, she was horrified. 'I never felt exploited by the director when I was actually making the film, but I definitely felt exploited when I watched it,' she told Munn (1997, p. 83). She goes on to say that she and Verhoeven had 'a big fight over it'; she asked him to remove the shot and he refused.

Verhoeven recalled the circumstances surrounding the shooting of the notorious scene very differently: he remembered talking the scene over with Stone in some detail both before and after filming it. In his interview with Linda Ruth Williams, he even recalls discussing it with her over dinner, recounting the story of his girlfriend from his student days, and notes that when Sharon heard it, 'her eyes lit up with diabolical pleasure, because she saw that was such a great idea' (Williams, 2005, p. 246). Verhoeven believes that one of the reasons that the scene became so famous was because Sharon Stone made such a fuss over it in the publicity surrounding the film's release, and, on this point, Eszterhas sides with Verhoeven. In *Hollywood Animal*, he refers to the conflicting accounts, and in particular Stone's denials: 'I knew what Sharon was doing and she was doing it well,' he wrote.

> She didn't want to be forever known for showing the world her pubes; she considered herself, after all, a serious actress. No one needed to know that, the morning she had shot *that* scene, she had handed her scented panties to Paul and said, 'I won't be needing these today.' (Eszterhas, 2005, p. 547)

Whatever the truth of the matter might be, the shooting of the scene itself was delayed until the end of the day, so that some degree of privacy could be maintained. The DVD commentary finds de Bont and Verhoeven clear and unanimous in their belief that Stone was fully aware of what was going on. 'If you put a camera between someone's legs and you have a little light there, it's most likely that you will see something,' de Bont remarks, with a chuckle. 'We had video standby all the time and she checked the shots out,' insists Verhoeven. Of course, DVD commentary tracks are not necessarily authoritative and should be assessed with a degree of scepticism: Neal King notes that they can be used by film-makers as a way to 'control the interpretations of their products […]. Public commentary, offered alongside the movies themselves, amounts to a marketing discourse of its own' (2004, pp. 2, 19). As so often, it becomes very difficult to parse the hype from the facts of the matter.

Filming the centrepiece sex scene between Tramell and Curran took three full days (Williams, 2005, p. 243), and seems to have been exhausting for both actors. In an interview for *Playboy* magazine, Stone pointed out that the 'athletic feat[s]' the storyboards required had necessitated 'serious fitness training', in particular the act of bending backwards and then pulling herself back up again without using her hands. 'It took some training to get my quadriceps strong enough so that I could manage it,' she remarked. 'I also had to be flexible enough to be able to do it fifty billion times so we could do all the takes' she added (Sheff, 1992). At the same time, she was rather dismissive and scornful about the sex scenes, particularly in response to suggestions that some of the sex may have been unsimulated. 'I didn't have a lot of input into the sex scenes', she told Sheff.

> Paul and Michael, very macho men, created them. When I read them and saw the storyboards, I thought they were ludicrous … . Do you have sex like that? Do you know women who have orgasms from these anatomically impossible positions? Please. In two minutes? Send them over to my house so I can learn. (Sheff, 1992)

Stone was also aware that there was a large measure of male fantasy and macho hubris involved:

> Once I realized that was what the guys wanted, I thought, Oh, I get it! No matter how he touches her or where he touches her or what else he does to her, it's the most, it's the best, it's the sexiest! … . I want to have some more of that! That's 'the fuck of the century,' according to the macho man mentality. (Sheff, 1992)

It is no surprise to find that accounts of the filming itself have always emphasised the choreographed nature of the action. According to Verhoeven, 'It's all extremely stylized, of course, and heavily storyboarded and extremely precisely edited' (quoted in Bouzereau, 1994, p. 201). Available excerpts from the storyboards endorse this position: they are extremely detailed, itemising each shot and camera angle, as well as camera movement.[7]

Verhoeven has always insisted that the nudity and explicit sexuality were not the *raisons d'être* of the scenes. In particular, the key love scene between Catherine and Nick was only possible in terms of the amount of nudity on show because, Verhoeven argues, it was also at the same time 'a thriller scene', with a number of visual cues (the mirror, the bed, the scarf) 'signalling to the audience that, yes, they're making love, but is she going to kill him or not?' (Williams, 2005, p. 243). At the same time, he also admits that 'it was always the idea for me to make the ultimate sex-scene' and that the scene between Nick and Catherine was certainly intended to be arousing (Williams, 2005, pp. 243–4). The MPAA would judge that he had achieved this particular aim, and a detailed discussion of the scene, assessing its structure, impact and the edits demanded by the MPAA, with a comparison of the cut and uncut versions, follows in Part 3.

… 'And Live Happily Ever After?'

The ending of *Basic Instinct* seems to have gone through a number of script changes, or posited options. Draft script pages include one ending that culminates with Catherine's death: in this version, which surely owes something to the *noir* classic *Double Indemnity* (1944), Catherine pulls a gun on Nick as they are locked in an embrace; she tells him she loves him, and squeezes the trigger, but before she can fire the shot, Nick stabs her in the heart with an ice-pick. 'I love you, too,' he replies, but, as her eyes glass over, Nick seems emotionless. The script tells us that 'Her body rests on his feet. His feet pull out from under her dead weight. The feet walk out of frame' (cited in Keesey and Duncan, 2005, p. 133). This version ends with the camera fixed on Catherine's body lying 'in a growing puddle of blood'. A second version, indicated by Verhoeven's thumbnail sketches next to the dialogue, sticks more closely to the final ending as shot, with Catherine and Nick making love, and then having their 'rugrats' conversation as they lie in bed. This time, however, as Nick turns away from her to stub out his cigarette, Catherine reaches for the ice-pick and, after she whispers, 'I love you', they kiss. The sketches indicate that the film fades to black just as we see a close-up of Catherine raising the ice-pick, with Nick's arms coming up to defend himself.

The first alternative ending is a disappointingly obvious cliché; at the same time, it would have been a suitably *noir*-ish conclusion; the original *film noir* movies would frequently have neutralized the sexual threat of the *femme fatale* by the time the closing credits ran, either by killing her, taming her or otherwise containing her subversive potential. However, as I will argue in Part 5, one of the reasons why *Basic Instinct* has exerted such a fascination over audiences, critics and academics is because Catherine Tramell represents a break from that tradition, and remains a powerful and inscrutable figure right up to the film's final frame, unshackled by conviction for her crimes, death or domestication. In the original script, during the final sequence, Eszterhas noted that the Rolling Stones' 'Sympathy for the Devil' should be playing, and the original intention was to bring the film to its conclusion while the Stones' song crescendoed to a dramatic climax (Eszterhas has said that he played their music constantly while working on the script, 'Sympathy for the Devil' in particular). Although the rights were paid for the song, it was not used; Verhoeven says he wanted to use it in the movie, but 'it didn't work' (Bouineau, 2001, p. 88). Nevertheless, the idea of Catherine as the devil is something that Verhoeven has cited frequently in interviews, and the ending as shot – even with the unambiguous attack on Nick exchanged for an embrace – reinforces that concept, with Nick deeply in Catherine's thrall, and the ice-pick patiently biding its time. 'Catherine Tramell is the Devil', Verhoeven told Bouineau; 'She's a human being, fully human, but she's also devilishly divine.' He goes on to muse that the fact that she does not kill Nick at the end of the film doesn't mean she won't kill him in due time: 'He's a dumb guy and she's in control. You cannot beat the devil' (2001, p. 88).

Unlike many Hollywood movies, the decision about the ending was not influenced by test screenings. Verhoeven claims there was no time to arrange them, and that, in any case, 'We didn't feel that it was necessary. Nobody asked, in fact. Nobody ever talked about it' (Bouzereau, 1994, p. 212). Verhoeven is convinced that, had they tested the film, the audiences would have expressed deep dissatisfaction with the ambiguity of the ending, and he would then have been under pressure to deliver a more straightforward conclusion, with either Nick or Catherine ending up dead. 'I wanted people to feel that ambiguity,' he told Bouzereau (1994, p. 213). As it would turn out, audience response to the ending would be the least of Verhoeven's worries. By the time he was shooting these scenes, there were already much bigger issues to confront than the prospect of disgruntled audiences.

✖ Part 2

PROTESTING *BASIC INSTINCT*

Production and Protests: The Context

Basic Instinct had had a troubled genesis, but much worse was to come. In February 1991 a version of the script had leaked and found its way into the hands of gay and lesbian pressure groups, notably GLAAD, Queer Nation and ACT UP (AIDS Coalition to Unleash Power), and a storm was gathering. It began with one meeting of about a dozen activists in West Hollywood, expressing their dismay not only at the representation of the bisexual killer but also, more vociferously, at the so-called date-rape scene in the script (Nick assaulting Beth). From here, the protest spread, with volunteers from a number of gay, lesbian and feminist groups faxing 250 newspapers, complaining about the negative representation of homosexuality in the film (Ellicott, 1992). Within days, an issue that began with a discussion among a small group of individuals would mushroom into the biggest Hollywood story of the year, and one of the most remarkable instances of grassroots censorship in US film history.

An understanding of the historical context for the trouble stirred by *Basic Instinct* is useful in providing a sense of perspective. Without it, the *Basic Instinct* controversy can seem like a curious anomaly – what Verhoeven tried to dismiss at the Cannes Film Festival as 'a storm in a glass of water' (Maslin, 1992b). Hollywood's 'celluloid closet' – its history of representation and (more often) repression of depictions of homosexuality – has been well documented, notably by Vito Russo (1987) and Harry M. Benshoff and Sean Griffin (2004). Charles Lyons briefly charts the same history in his discussion of *Basic Instinct*'s place in the culture wars of the 1990s, noting the significance of the Kinsey Report, which opened a window on America's bedrooms and exposed the gap between what was spoken about and what was done in terms of sexuality. Lyons also notes the conflation of homosexuality with Communism during the era of

McCarthyism, and the insistence of the MPAA and CARA on retaining the categorisation of homosexuality as a form of sexual deviance (Lyons, 1997, pp. 110–13). By the late 1960s and early 1970s, homosexuality was beginning to feature far more heavily in mainstream film; at the same time, despite the work of activists striving for an end to discrimination and victimisation of gays and lesbians, negative stereotypes were persistent and proliferating. The key precedent for the trouble that *Basic Instinct* ran into was William Friedkin's *Cruising*. The activism that Verhoeven's project would provoke followed a similar pattern to the protests that erupted around Friedkin's.

Cruising was adapted from Gerald Walker's 1970 novel and told the story of an undercover cop (Al Pacino) on the trail of a serial killer in New York City's gay community, in particular the S&M subculture. Just as would happen ten years later, a draft of the script leaked and co-founder of the National Gay Task Force, Arthur Bell, lambasted it in a *Village Voice* article, predicting that the film would prove to be 'the most oppressive, ugly, bigoted look at homosexuality ever presented on the screen'. Bell encouraged all his readers, 'gay, straight, liberal, radical, atheist, communist, or whatever' to do all they could to disrupt the filming (Bell cited in Sandler, 2007, pp. 66–7). Attempts were made to persuade the producer and director to make script changes to present a more balanced representation of homosexuals and their lifestyles. When these attempts were rebuffed, activists organised a march through Greenwich Village, while the Mayor, Ed Koch, was lobbied to withdraw the film-makers' permit, a request he refused. Further protests and demonstrations followed, with significant disruption to the shooting of the movie. As would be the case with *Basic Instinct*, the controversy developed into a rhetorical battle invoking the Constitution and accusations of censorship. Ronald Gold of the National Gay Task Force had a smart rejoinder to such charges, however: 'Nobody would dare to do a film about a group of organized black men whose objective is to rape a white woman,' he pointed out. 'We always find ourselves in a position of having to play civil libertarian to a bunch of bigots who want their constitutional right to express their hatred of us' (cited in Lyons, 1997, p. 119). Friedkin did eventually make one concession of a kind that Verhoeven would adamantly refuse: a disclaimer in *Cruising*'s closing credits read, 'This film is not intended as an indictment of the homosexual world. It is set in one small segment of that world which is not meant to be representative of the whole' (Lyons, 1997, p. 122).

If the first half of the 1980s saw the start of a shift – Lyons notes the appearance of more varied and positive representations of homosexuality in films like *Personal Best* (1982), *La Cage aux Folles* (1984), the British film *My Beautiful Laundrette* (1986) and others – the emergence of AIDS into the cultural mainstream in the second half of the decade seemed to reset the agenda. Lyons singles out the attempts to suppress the homoerotic art of Robert Mapplethorpe as a key flashpoint, but this was part of a much wider sociocultural shift in a period characterised by a rising sense of panic as the epidemic spread. It would seem that in the wake of this cultural turn, Hollywood opted to play safe. *Longtime Companion* (1989), a chronicle of the impact of the disease on a group of gay men in New York, stood virtually alone as a major film willing to explore the issues with compassion and understanding, but it was an independent production partly funded by PBS (Public Broadcasting Service). According to gay activists, Hollywood's reticence was simply a reflection of 'a strong undercurrent of homophobia in the movie community', which had also led actors of both orientations to 'shun overtly gay roles for fear of hurting their careers' (Simpson, 1992, p. 65). In society at large, in the wake of what was identified in the first instance as a 'gay plague' (until it began to spread more widely and rapidly among drug abusers and the urban poor), there was a rise in instances of violence directed against homosexuals: 'A five-city survey conducted by the National Gay and Lesbian Task Force Policy Institute reports a 31% increase in gay-bashing incidents, including a jump in the number of anti-gay murders to eight, from three in 1990' (Simpson, 1992, p. 65).

Another element in the cultural turn at the end of the 1980s was undoubtedly the influence of the Religious Right on public attitudes and debate. During the 80s, the Religious Right had become a significant political force, increasingly aligned with the Republican Party, although the alliance would begin to split towards the end of George Bush Sr's presidency. Staunchly opposed to abortion and gay rights in particular, the Religious Right was perturbed by Bush's shift towards a more moderate stand on both issues, the latter crystallised in a row over funding from the National Endowment for the Arts (NEA). Incensed by the President's refusal to intervene in the row over the funding of exhibitions it perceived as sacrilegious (Andres Serrano's 'Piss Christ') and homoerotic and pornographic (Robert Mapplethorpe's photography), the Religious Right became increasingly strident as it expressed its dissatisfaction with what it saw as Bush's weakness.[8]

At the same time that those at one end of the sociopolitical and cultural spectrum were demanding more attention for their deeply conservative views, gay and lesbian pressure groups were proliferating, partly as a response to the AIDS epidemic and its repercussions. Tina Fetner notes that the greater organisation and coordination of these groups had been developed partly as a result of the support networks that had been set up to deal with AIDS victims, particularly in the wake of the failure of the federal health system to respond adequately to the crisis (Fetner, 2008, pp. 51–6). GLAAD, whose West Hollywood chapter would spark the protest against *Basic Instinct*, was founded in 1985 in New York City, and the first activists were led to form their protest group in response to the coverage of gay issues in the *New York Post*, particularly with regard to AIDS-related news items. In 1987, a National March on Washington for Lesbian and Gay Rights drew 650,000 demonstrators. GLAAD's high-profile protest against Bob Hope's off-the-cuff homophobic remark on the popular *Johnny Carson Show* on national television – a protest that resulted in Hope filming a public-service announcement denouncing violence against homosexuals as reparation (Nardi and Bolton, 1998, p. 412) – first brought it widespread attention in 1988, but the *Basic Instinct* protests would cause even more of a stir.

Protesting *Basic Instinct*

Basic Instinct was set in and around San Francisco and the Bay Area –
Eszterhas's adopted home. San Francisco has probably the largest
concentration of same-sex couples in the US, and was well known for its
active and vocal gay and lesbian organisations. This tradition of activism was
due in part to the high profile of Harvey Milk, an openly gay politician elected
to serve on the board of supervisors in San Francisco in 1977, shot dead by an
anti-gay conservative board member the following year.[9] In the 1980s, as the
AIDS epidemic took a firm hold on the headlines, the gay community became
increasingly politicised, partly through necessity in response to an increase in
homophobia in the United States. Hollie Conley of the San Francisco chapter
of GLAAD believed *Basic Instinct* was 'dangerous … in the current climate',
and expressed grave concern that

> the extraordinary level of street violence against gays in the US is being
> fuelled by Hollywood films that repeatedly portray gay men and lesbians
> as psychopathic, deranged or subhuman, and that studios are unwilling
> to allow any other images into mainstream cinema. (Alcorn, 1991, p. 17)

Richard Goldstein, writing in the *Village Voice*, suggested, with a touch of
irony, that the negative representations of homosexuals in films such as *JFK*
(1991), *The Silence of the Lambs* (1991) and *Basic Instinct* ('man-haters
with ice-pick dicks') 'may actually quiet the anxieties of heterosexuals'.
Acknowledging the impact of the Religious Right on public discourse,
Goldstein mused, 'Each of these clichés affirms that queers are as socially
destructive as [Republican Presidential candidate] Pat Buchanan says, yet
each is a product of Hollywood's liberal establishment' (Goldstein cited in
Appiah, 1993, p. 86).

     There was a significant groundswell among gay activists who felt
increasing levels of tension and frustration at what was perceived to be
Hollywood's latent homophobia. For Christopher Sharrett, *Basic Instinct*, like

The Hand That Rocks the Cradle (1992) and *Fatal Attraction*, was part of a clear agenda, 'an attempt to warn the audience to stay solidly within the bounds of monogamous, heterosexual relationships lest all hell break loose'. He continued: 'The AIDS message is packaged as a sort of neoconservative terrorism, especially as it depicts women, gays, and sexuality itself as inherently evil' (Sharrett, 1992, p. 93).

Hollie Conley of GLAAD pointed out in an interview for the *Guardian* that the recent Steve Martin comedy *LA Story* (1991) had had two positive lesbian characters removed from the film following negative reactions at test screenings, and that a sequence from the Blake Edwards comedy *Switch* (1991), in which a man wakes up in a female body, was cut because it depicted the protagonist in a love scene with another woman, a former girlfriend (Alcorn, 1991, p. 17). In September 1990, the LA chapter of GLAAD had taken out advertisements in both *Daily Variety* and the *Hollywood Reporter*, asking producers, 'Where are the lesbian and gay characters this season? We are tired of seeing gays represented only as buffoons or villains' (Alcorn, 1991, p. 17). At the time they were interviewed by Alcorn, they were also planning a March on Hollywood in January the following year, to include 'coming out parties' for dead film stars such as Gary Cooper. If some saw the objections as overly zealous political correctness, for others it was a long overdue redressing of the balance: 'I think communities demanding a positive representation in the arts and voicing their opinions at the negative portrayals will become one of the decade's major issues,' Michelangelo Signorile of New York's *Outweek* magazine remarked (Alcorn, 1991, p. 17).

Rick Ruvolo, a legal aide to San Francisco City Supervisor Harry Britt, summed up the gay community's objections to the film: 'The good guy is a straight white male and all the bad people are bisexual women and lesbians who have a history of hating men and killing them. And it's not only homophobic, it's anti-woman', he continued. 'Imagine a rape scene in which a woman kisses a man goodbye and thanks him after he forces her to have sex' (Smith, 1991).[10] The protesters viewed the film as one 'that once again inverts the realities of our lives' (*Time*, 1991, p. 70). Jonathan Katz, founder of Queer

Nation, saw the character of Catherine Tramell as the next in a 'long line' of the tradition of 'the homicidal evil lesbian'.[11] Fellow activist Annette Gaudino noted how, as usual, 'the real lesbian [Roxy] ends up dead' while the bisexual Catherine ends up with a man, and that 'queer sexuality and violence were clearly linked'.[12] 'Every lesbian and bisexual character in these films is accused of being a psychotic killer,' said Kate Sorensen of Queer Nation. 'And the girl never gets the girl. I'm tired of that' (Simpson, 1992). The GLAAD statement released about the time shooting began insisted that, 'The film industry bears a grave responsibility for the perpetuation of stereotypes and the dramatic increase in homophobic violence over the past few years' (van Scheers, 1997, p. 247). What followed is an excellent example of grassroots censorship in action.

According to Charles Lyons's detailed account, the organised strategy of protest against the shooting of *Basic Instinct* began in February with a letter-writing campaign asking Carolco to either drop the film entirely, or at least to shoot it outside San Francisco (Lyons, 1997, p. 126). One of the chosen locations, a gay country-and-western bar called The Rawhide II, was vandalised and the owner, Ray Chalker, complained of 'threats on my voice mail, constant harassment, Super Glue put into the locks of my home and vandalism to my $80,000 Mercedes' (Fox and Rosenthal, 1991). At the same time, 'Kill Ray' posters began appearing in gay neighbourhoods (Leo, 1992, p. 24). On 10 April 1991, Queer Nation staged a demonstration at the site where preparations for exterior shooting were being made, and over the following weeks, they stepped up their action, picketing locations and shouting and chanting to try and cause maximum disruption to cast and crew. The impact of the protests on the progress of the production was considerable: although an attempt to disrupt the filming of the car chase was less successful (such scenes do not rely on a live recorded soundtrack), the activity certainly slowed things down and incurred some significant extra costs. Some temporary sets were daubed with paint, necessitating a shift of location and redecoration; cables were cut and protesters flashed torches at the cameras during filming. In the midst of this, the mayor of San Francisco Art

Agnos, up for re-election at the time, weighed into the controversy by issuing a statement that perched somewhat precariously on the fence, agreeing with the protesters' objections to the film about negative images of homosexuality in the movie, but insisting that he could not allow the city to be put 'in the position of censoring a movie script. Nor should we be giving a Jesse Helms-like seal of approval to programs or scripts', he added, referencing the infamous Senator from North Carolina renowned for his racist, homophobic and socially conservative attitudes (Fox and Rosenthal, 1991).

Time magazine suggested the controversy needed to be understood in the context of other minority groups protesting over their representation in Hollywood movies: African Americans as criminals, Arab Americans as terrorists, Native Americans as savages. 'Now gay activists are taking to the streets to decry the growing number of movies that, they say, are stereotyping them as psychopathic killers' (Simpson, 1992). One activist claimed that a direct link was visible between negative portrayals of gays and lesbians in Hollywood film and alarming rises in instances of homophobic attacks. According to Carol Anderson of the Gay and Lesbian Alliance, 'We have been seeing an increase in gay bashing in the last several years, and also an increase in the negative depiction of gays in movies.' The same thinking underpinned some of the later protest campaigns; the group christening itself 'Catherine Did It!' was very clear about the link, as it perceived it, between real life and representation: 'The sensationalized depictions of lesbians and gays that Hollywood has always served up to the public are not fiction, they are fraud', their statement declared. 'But the hatred they perpetuate and the pain they cause to many innocent people is very real' (Kauffman, 1992, p. 37).

Summit Meeting

Finally, in an attempt to find a way forward, a meeting was set up between the activists and the film's creative team: Eszterhas, Verhoeven and producer Alan Marshall. In attendance at that meeting at the San Francisco Hyatt Hotel on

24 April were city officials and members of a number of pressure groups, including the National Organization for Women (NOW), Community United Against Violence, Queer Nation and ACT UP. The protesters set their sights high: they demanded a number of key script changes, and vowed that, if their demands were not met, they would make sure that filming would not continue in San Francisco. Jonathan Katz of the Queer Nation group, which was generally more militant than GLAAD (Lyons, 1997, p. 126), declared, 'Not unless the script is completely rewritten and the premise changed, will we stop demonstrating. We have the shooting schedule of the film, and we'll really go into action while they're shooting on public streets' (Fox and Rosenthal, 1991). The activists pinpointed all the dialogue that they deemed anti-gay or anti-lesbian. More audaciously, they requested that Michael Douglas's character be recast as a lesbian (even going so far as to suggest Kathleen Turner for the role), and that either the gender of the killer be switched, or else that Catherine and Roxy both murder a couple of women in order to redress the balance and subvert the stereotype of the psychotic, man-hating lesbian killer – the issue that was clearly at the heart of their objections to the movie.

Once again, the film's purported homophobia was not the only target; protesters were also outraged by the contentious sex scene involving Nick and Beth. According to the *New York Times*, 'members of the National Organization for Women were concerned in particular about a "date-rape" scene in which the woman ends up thanking her rapist' (Lew, 1991). Tammy Bruce, a representative of the Los Angeles branch of NOW, remarked that, 'We were expecting it to be homophobic, but it is also one of the most misogynistic films in recent memory' (Johnson and Dwyer, 1992).

Accounts of the meeting vary considerably. According to Verhoeven, he, Marshall, Eszterhas and Douglas had agreed before going into the meeting that they would hold a united line against the protests. Verhoeven in particular was as adamant that nothing would be altered as he had been about making changes to the original screenplay in his early battles with Eszterhas and Winkler. The director was uncompromising from the moment the meeting started, determined that he would make no concessions to what he saw as politically correct censorship. His intransigence clearly angered the protesters. However, over the course of the meeting, Eszterhas seemed to capitulate and agreed to rework the script to take account of some of the activists' objections. According to Eszterhas's own account in his autobiography *Hollywood Animal,* he lined himself up, literally and metaphorically, on the side of the protesters from the beginning of the meeting, choosing to sit among them, facing Verhoeven, Marshall and the other studio representatives.

The meeting gave Eszterhas considerable food for thought. In particular, he was impressed by supervisor Harry Britt: 'I found him a very sensitive, intelligent, interesting man and not a militant at all,' said Eszterhas. 'So when he took offence to certain pieces of dialogue I was willing to change it' (van Scheers, 1997, p. 248). He disagreed with the protesters on a number of points: their characterisation of Tramell as a lesbian was, he believed, problematic, arguing that Catherine and Roxy were both *bisexual*, not lesbians. On the other hand, some of the abusive language (such as Gus's reference to 'dykes') was, he felt on reflection, unnecessary, and he agreed to look at those parts of the script again. However, the production was already three weeks into the shoot, and Eszterhas was now attempting to rewrite a number of scenes and recast a part; it was clear to any disinterested observer that this was going to be unworkable. Eszterhas claimed that the alterations were necessary, to 'reflect the sensitivities expressed by the gay community leaders. In my mind', he told a *New York Times* reporter, 'these are changes that are very important in the perception of gay people and women in our society' (Lew, 1991). He claimed that the revisions would result in 'a more socially responsible and creative movie'. However, others in the industry reportedly viewed him as a 'slippery opportunist who ha[d] changed sides in the debate for politically correct reasons', and because he feared for the safety of his wife and children, in the wake of some of the more vehement protests (Greig, 1992, p.13).

The series of changes that he sent to Verhoeven, Eszterhas felt, 'violated neither the story nor the characters' (Eszterhas, 2005, p. 303) and, very reluctantly, Verhoeven agreed to look at his writer's proposals. In the end, none of the changes were major structural ones – the gender and casting switches the protesters had demanded were ignored. However, the revisions were still substantial: there were thirty-seven in all (Ellicott, 1992, p.1), centring almost exclusively on the dialogue, removing potentially offensive references to homosexuals and lesbians, and inserting a line in which Nick rebuffs a homophobic remark made by his partner Gus: 'A lot of the best people I've met in this town are gay.' In his director's commentary, Verhoeven gives another example of the proposed changes: [13] when Nick wants to know why Beth did not reveal her history with Catherine when she was first brought in for questioning, Beth is scornful, asking Nick what he expected her to say: 'Hey guys, I'm not gay but I did fuck your suspect?' she suggests, sarcastically. She excuses herself by explaining that she was 'embarrassed'; she continues, 'It was the only time I had been with a woman.' In his commentary, Verhoeven recites the text the protesters wanted to replace the original lines with:

Beth: What was I supposed to say, hey guys, I fucked your suspect? I'm bisexual. [They look at each other.] Does that matter to you that I'm bisexual?
Nick: No, it does not.
Beth: Well, it would matter to a lot of people.
Nick: Well, it doesn't matter to me.

It is not very difficult to understand why Verhoeven was reluctant to incorporate such clumsy concessions to very specific cultural sensitivities into the shooting script.

However, Eszterhas's rewrite did include a small number of more substantial changes: the sex scene between Beth and Nick that the activists had attacked as an example of date rape would be turned into a straightforward love scene. More significantly, he proposed that two of the murder victims should be women instead of men 'in order to show that the killer is not acting from a man-hating rage but from a psychopathic illness … her violence is directed at both men and women' (quoted in Lyons, 1997, p. 128). He also wanted a disclaimer screened, *Cruising*-style, at the start of the film advising that, 'The movie you are about to see is fiction. Its gay and bisexual characters are fictional and not based on reality' (van Scheers, 1997, p. 248).

Having reviewed Eszterhas's revisions, on 30 April the production team rejected them wholesale. The statement declared that they would 'undermine the strength of Eszterhas's original material, weaken the characters which he so vividly portrayed, and lessen the integrity of the picture itself' (Lew, 1991). Marshall, Verhoeven and Douglas all saw Eszterhas's volte-face as a betrayal. 'Joe claimed it was a matter of principle,' Douglas remarked, 'and now we know this man has no principles' (Greig, 1992, p. 26). Carolco backed them up, with President and CEO of the company, Peter Hoffman, telling *Vanity Fair* that the changes were 'patronizing drivel', Eszterhas 'a sniveling hypocrite', and asserting that Carolco would 'never change a script in response to political pressure' (Lyons, 1997, pp. 128–9). Besides, Verhoeven would argue later, many of the protests were based on a 'misinterpretation' of the screenplay: 'They saw a blueprint for a movie, and out of that blueprint they started to construct their own house', he complained. 'But it was not the house that I was going to build. It is very difficult to read a script. It is like reading a score without knowing notes' (McGregor, 1992, p. 20).

'Political Correctness' and Free Speech

The irony of the situation was not lost on Eszterhas: having first walked away from the film because the director wanted to change his script, he was ready to do the same again because Verhoeven would not accept any changes to a screenplay the director had first tried to rewrite himself, before admitting it was better the way it had been in the first place. Once again Eszterhas abandoned the project in protest. For this, he earned the praise of at least some of those who had objected to the film: Chris Fowler of GLAAD in Los Angeles told Alex McGregor that 'We think Joe showed a lot of sensitivity about our complaints. He made it clear that he wasn't interested in anything that was anti-gay' (McGregor, 1992, p. 21). As for the stars, who were protected to a degree from the protesters' vehement hostility, it was impossible for them to avoid the controversy entirely, or refrain from commenting on it, either during shooting or later in interviews promoting the film. Michael Douglas, who had a considerable financial stake in the movie, seems to have been somewhat perplexed by the activists: 'There we were, making what was meant to be a little psycho thriller and all of a sudden we were of sociological importance .... It was just wild' (van Scheers, 1997, p. 249). At the time, Douglas appeared to be bemused by the reaction to the 'date-rape' scene. 'That was not a rape,' he protested. 'It was aggressive sex between adults. Are these people now telling us that aggressive sex is not allowed? This is getting ridiculous' (O'Sullivan, 1992).

In her interview with David Sheff for *Playboy* in December 1992, Sharon Stone was more expansive, even if her logic was occasionally hard to follow. 'I never had any problems with the gay community,' she said, noting how 'many of my dating experiences included me and my date and a gay couple. It was very much the norm.' As a consequence, she claimed to be 'sensitive to issues that would concern gay people. That's why the flap over *Basic Instinct* was beyond my comprehension,' she continued. 'My perspective of my lesbian relationship in the film was that it was a pure, loving relationship. At the same time, Catherine was clearly not a lesbian. She was a party girl' (Sheff, 1992).

It may not be entirely fair to parse a remark made in an interview too closely, but a certain amount of discomfort is inescapable amid the background noise: what is to all intents and purposes a 'some of my best friends are gay' defence is followed up by some contradictory statements about Stone's character: while in a 'lesbian relationship' she describes as 'pure' and 'loving' (what does 'pure' signify in this context?), she is 'clearly not a lesbian' but 'a party girl'. Presumably this means that Catherine is the kind of character who will take pleasure where she can find it, whether that be with men or women, which begs a number of questions: why does Stone seem reluctant to label Catherine as bisexual? And how does the 'party-girl' characterisation relate to that 'pure, loving relationship'? In the same interview, Stone took a different line from Douglas's notes of perplexity and impatience: remarking that the making of the film was 'a unique opportunity for the gay community to use a big media event as a way to be heard', she concluded: 'That was good. I'm enormously sympathetic with the issue that was raised' (Sheff, 1992).

Douglas's reactions generally betray a greater sense of impatience, and a more confrontational attitude. 'To me this is a sign of how lost this country is[,] how it has no direction and everyone is floundering, hanging on to their own special interests.' In admitting to being 'out of touch with this crowd objecting to Basic Instinct' (O'Sullivan, 1992), Douglas is not ceding ground, but rather identifying himself with a wider backlash against efforts on several fronts to establish greater equality for minority groups, and reduce discrimination at every level: political, economic, social and cultural. Indeed, some of his remarks fit very comfortably with the star persona he had cultivated, one 'built on making explicit some of the contradictions and multivalencies in constructions of white masculinity' (Davies and Smith, 1997, p. 25). In an interview with *GQ* magazine, the target of Douglas's wrath was identified much more unequivocally: 'I've always supported gay rights. But this whole thing of being politically correct is really a bore. In movies somebody's got to be the villain', he quipped, 'And it can't always be the Italians' (Austin, 2002, p. 57). Paul Brett, director of Marketing at Guild Film Distribution, invoked the same argument: the idea that 'politically correct' attitudes militate against the constitutional right to freedom of expression. Brett dismissed the idea that gays 'should only be shown in "normal" roles and never portrayed as villains. If that was the case,' he argued, 'we'd only have white male Protestant villains.' He went on to denounce political correctness as 'censorship of the worst kind' (*Empire,* 1992, p. 6). In other interviews, Verhoeven presented what could be described as a more reasoned defence. A writer for the Canadian current-affairs magazine *Maclean's* pointed out that his homoerotic thriller *The Fourth Man* had been well received by the gay community. Verhoeven agreed, suggesting to *Maclean's* another perspective on the controversy: 'Homosexuality is a part of life,' he told the reporter. 'You can make it a plot point without making it an issue all the time' (Johnson and Dwyer, 1992).

Basic Instinct and Homophobia

On sober reflection, and with the benefit of some twenty years of hindsight, what is one to make today of the charges laid against *Basic Instinct* by the gay and lesbian pressure groups? They accused the film of perpetuating negative stereotypes of bisexuals and lesbians, in particular the association of lesbianism with psychosis. They protested at the representation of Roxy in particular, and the narrative arc for her character. They also objected strongly to the so-called 'date-rape' scene involving Nick and Beth.

It is true to say that all the key female characters in the movie are psychologically disturbed, and that most of them have committed acts of extreme violence. Accepting that Catherine is the murderess, we watch her kill Johnny Boz and Gus, and we can assume she was also responsible for the deaths of her parents, her college professor Goldstein and the Internal Affairs officer Nilsen. Hazel Dobkins is an ex-convict who was jailed for slaughtering her family; Roxy, in a jealous rage, threatens to kill Nick and later attempts to run him down in her car; we hear a short time later that when she was younger, Roxy killed her two brothers with her father's razor. By the end of the film, the audience is presumably meant to assume Beth is innocent, but we have already witnessed a couple of frenzied outbursts on her part, and we have heard that she had developed an unhealthy obsession with Catherine during their time at college together. A question mark remains over the death of her husband, even after the hurried untangling of plot knots has cleared her of Gus's murder. Furthermore, the homicides committed by the women are all characterised as particularly disturbing precisely *because* of their apparent lack of purpose, motivation or rationale: when Gus recalls the murders committed by Hazel Dobkins, he tells Nick that he 'couldn't get it out of [his] head for years':

> Nice little housewife, three little kids, nice husband, wasn't porking around, no financial problems. One day out of the clear blue sky she does 'em. All of 'em. Used a knife she got for a wedding present. Didn't even deny it. Sweet as honey. Said she didn't know why she'd done it.

The implication is that violent women are in this sense doubly 'unnatural': not only is it shocking to see or hear of women committing murder, the nature of their crimes makes them even more disturbing. With this in mind, it is not surprising that the film was accused by many of its critics of perpetuating the 'killer-lesbian' stereotype that Vito Russo identifies in his book *The Celluloid Closet* (1987).[14]

John Weir asks the pertinent question, what is the point of Catherine's lesbianism?

> It explains nothing about her. Her relationships with other women are sketchily dramatized. Roxy, the film's totemic lesbian, is dispensed with summarily in an obligatory car chase. (And Catherine, who finds herself in bed with Nick only hours later, barely mourns her passing.) Dorothy Malone has a virtually silent role as another female killer [Dobkins]. She submits to a vague caress from Catherine and then disappears. In 'Basic Instinct,' lesbianism isn't an orientation, or even a life style. It's a plot point. It gets Nick confused about who murdered whom. And it implies villainy. (Weir, 1992)

Galvin believes that Catherine is 'clearly placed as an object of male fantasy ahead of lesbian or heterosexual female identification' (Galvin, 1994, p. 231), and Clare Whatling agrees: 'Wherever lesbians appear outside of the feminist avant-garde, they do so as a function of male voyeurism', referring to 'the mainstream sleaze of Paul Verhoeven's *Basic Instinct*' as a good example (Whatling, 1997, p. 104). Thomas Austin's audience research on the film seems to bear this out, with many respondents to his survey 'afford[ing] primacy to the sight of the female body. 'These accounts', he continues, 'typically suppressed the narrative agency of Catherine in favour of positioning her as erotic object' (Austin, 1999, p. 150).

It is easy to perceive the film's lesbianism as a familiar play for the attentions of the typical male heterosexual cinemagoer. Verhoeven's keen intention to alter Eszterhas's original screenplay by adding a lesbian love scene between Catherine and Roxy lends itself to just such an interpretation. Verhoeven felt that Eszterhas had neglected to include one because of some misguided sense of delicacy, and that the movie would be enhanced by it, presumably as much for the sake of breaking new ground in explicit representations of sex as for its potential significance to narrative or character development. In the end, Verhoeven conceded that the inclusion of such a scene would be counterproductive. Thus a film (in)famous for its inclusion of lesbians and bisexuals actually contains no lesbian sex scene, putting it at something of a disadvantage in the marketplace when compared to the endlessly proliferating direct-to-video erotic thrillers, where these scenes are a staple.

The movie does pander, presumably unwittingly, to other aspects of cultural homophobia. Beth's youthful infatuation with Catherine is treated in a clichéd fashion, with Beth insisting it was merely a phase ('I was embarrassed. It was the only time I had been with a woman'). In addition, some critics of the film's sexual politics have characterised Roxy's actions as behaviour associated with the stereotype of the man-hating woman (and the accusation is that the film assumes that, as a lesbian, Roxy naturally hates men). Verhoeven, in his commentary, is keen to point out that Roxy is evidently not going after Nick because she hates men as a group; the script is quite clear that Nick is her specific target. She is driven insane by the jealousy that has consumed her since she watched Catherine having sex with him. Nevertheless, as many others have pointed out, the psychotic lesbian – safely contained or more often than not killed off – is a hackneyed character type, and the rather obvious coding of Roxy as butch is also clumsy and stereotypical.

Disruption on Location

Regardless of any attempts by the stars themselves to bring about some kind of détente, the protests continued. The debate soon turned into a rhetorical battle about freedom of speech (Lyons, 1997, pp. 132–3), a debate which would return with a vengeance when the campaign to disrupt screenings of the film on its opening weekend began (see pp. 79–83). This chapter of the conflict between film-makers and activists was probably initiated by Carolco's statement following the meeting of 24 April. The company declared that, 'While these groups have a right to express their opinions, they have no right to threaten First Amendment guarantees of freedom of speech and expression' (Lyons, 1997, pp. 129–30). As so often in debates about freedom of speech, particularly in cases where the supposed left liberals find themselves cast in the role of censor, sensibilities were raw. The *San Francisco Examiner* described the protesters as 'the thought police of the left', and such accusations were in turn dismissed by the activists as examples of implicit homophobia: Rick Ruvolo responded that the real problem was 'institutional censorship that has censored gay men and lesbians for many years'; Hollie Conley of GLAAD similarly spoke of Hollywood's custom of 'mak[ing] movies that pander to people's homophobia'; for Conley, it was not a case of censorship but of 'social responsibility' (Lyons, 1997, p. 130).

One particularly large and loud gathering outside the Moscone Center[15] in downtown San Francisco, where exterior shooting had begun, shouted, yelled slogans and blew whistles in efforts to disrupt the filming. The next night, the protesters waved American flags and held up signs asking passing motorists to sound their horns to show their support for the US Army ('Honk if you support our boys in the Gulf'). According to Keith Alcorn, 'Filming had to be abandoned minutes later' (Alcorn, 1991, p. 17). The demonstrations continued night after night, with protesters confronting police in riot gear: Alan Marshall had managed to win a temporary restraining order barring the demonstrators from approaching the film set, although San Francisco Superior Court Judge John Dearman had decided on a 100-foot zone rather than the 200-yard limit that the film company had requested. Marshall claims that he was forced to make his own arrests when the police declared that the protesters were doing nothing unlawful. The restraining order was Marshall's, they said, and it was up to him to enforce it by nominating those that he wanted arrested. He subsequently netted twenty-six demonstrators on the first night. Most of the songs and chants the protesters came up with, Marshall believes, were aimed at him. He became a convenient hate figure for the focus of their demonstrations, which continued throughout the eighteen nights of location shooting.

There is no doubt that the gay and lesbian activists' coordinated protests against *Basic Instinct* raised awareness of the issue of representations of homosexuality in film at a time when sensitivity among these groups was markedly high. It is perhaps unsurprising that, in the end, the protesters were unable to effect the changes in the script that they demanded, or to disrupt the shooting of the movie to an extent that would do anything more than inconvenience the studio and its employees. Furthermore, the protesters ran the risk of alienating many neutral observers, who in a nation very much preoccupied with the right to freedom of speech, may not have appreciated what some sought to characterise as 'political correctness'. Nevertheless, this was not the end of the matter for the protesters. As the film moved from post-production into marketing and distribution, the next stage of their campaign would begin.

✖ Part 3

CENSORING *BASIC INSTINCT*

Certificates and Ratings

The reception of *Basic Instinct* at the offices of CARA was inevitably conditioned by the publicity that had surrounded it ever since Eszterhas first sold the script for a record fee. The conflict between director and writer, the protests that had disrupted the shooting of the movie, and in particular the rumours about the film's graphic sex scenes ensured that it would receive close scrutiny at the classification stage. And, following extended wrangling with the Rating Board, *Basic Instinct* would go on to stir another wave of protests, with gay and lesbian groups picketing cinemas across the country on its release. In the press, when the attention was not on GLAAD and its allies, the film would provoke movie critics to file some lively (and often decidedly mixed) reviews.

Regardless, the film was undoubtedly adventurous in terms of the boundaries Verhoeven saw fit to test, particularly with regard to sexual content. While it would cause little or no trouble in the UK, where BBFC policy meant that exhibition of the film could simply be restricted to adults via the 18 certificate, the case was more complicated in the US. As early as the start of the 1970s, the X rating, which restricted viewing first to those aged sixteen or older and then, from 1970, to those aged seventeen and over, had taken on quite specific connotations. Increasingly identified with pornography, it took only a couple of years for the major studios to begin giving the rating a very wide berth. Directors were left under no illusion that they would have to deliver cuts of their movies that the Rating Board, CARA, would be willing to pass at R (Restricted, meaning that those aged under seventeen had to be accompanied by an adult). By 1974, the major studios were releasing no X-rated films at all (Sandler, 2007, p. 63), leaving it in the domain of the independent studios (who used it sparingly) and the

UNIVERSITY OF WINCHESTER
LIBRARY

pornographers (who exploited it ruthlessly). Prompted in the first instance by film critics, chiefly in the wake of the ratings disputes over *The Cook, the Thief, His Wife and Her Lover* (1989) and *Tie Me Up! Tie Me Down!* (1990), the MPAA made a new, concerted effort to overhaul the X with the introduction of the NC-17 (no children under the age of seventeen admitted) in 1990. The first film to be certificated NC-17, *Henry and June* (1990), was the story of the love lives of authors Henry Miller and Anaïs Nin, including Nin's relationship with another woman. It was the Rating Board's refusal to allow the film's sex scenes (predominantly between women) through without cuts which effectively brought about the introduction of the new rating. An appeal against the decision to refuse it an R certificate uncut threatened to wreck the classification system entirely, or at least the industry's faith in it (see Sandler, 2007, pp. 111–13). Unfortunately, *Henry and June* was a commercial disappointment, grossing only $11.5 million, and the NC-17 initiative began to founder almost as soon as it was launched.

Not that the studios didn't try to find a way to make the rating changes work to their advantage, at least for a short while. Stephen Vaughn points out that a number of them were trying to generate buzz for mainstream films featuring graphic sex by performing elaborate dances around the line between R and NC-17, notably with Ken Russell's *Whore* (1991) and *Color of Night* (1994), which featured full frontal male nudity in the rather surprising shape of Bruce Willis. The latter would end up cut for R and take almost $20 million (still only half its budget); *Whore* was released as an NC-17 and grossed just over $1 million (boxofficemojo.com, 2012a). Other movies launched with the more restrictive rating at this time included art-house fare (*Prospero's Books* in 1991, *The Lover* in 1992, *Damage* in 1993), and a shameless *Basic Instinct* wannabe, the Madonna vehicle *Body of Evidence* (1993) (Vaughn, 2006, pp. 213–14). Cut for R, *Body of Evidence* would recoup only $13 million of its $30-million production budget on its theatrical release (boxofficemojo.com, 2012b).

According to Verhoeven, the MPAA was eager to persuade the studio to release *Basic Instinct* with an NC-17 rating. 'After showing the MPAA the first cut […], they said this is great, it's a wonderful movie, please don't change it, it's an NC-17', he told Laurent Bouzereau. 'They wanted a big audience movie to be NC-17 and still be a good movie, not a work of exploitation. They wanted to legitimize the NC-17' (Bouzereau, 1994, p. 206). Verhoeven estimated that an NC-17 *Basic Instinct* could have taken 'sixty or seventy' million dollars at the US box office, but Tri-Star and Carolco executives thought it would make half that (Bouzereau, 1994, p. 206). An NC-17 was therefore never a realistic option, and Verhoeven was well aware of the fact. However, the publicity that could be generated by appearing to hesitate over the issue was obvious.

Henry and June may have been a commercial failure, as well as a failed experiment for the MPAA, but it still stands in second place in the box-office returns for all NC-17 films ever released. The pride of first place belongs to Verhoeven and Eszterhas though not courtesy of *Basic Instinct*. In 1995, they would collaborate on *Showgirls*. Set in Vegas, the film tracks the progress of starlet Nomi (Elizabeth Berkley) as she attempts to establish herself as a high-class showgirl, following her on her way through lap-dancing clubs towards the big time. In Rob van Scheers's words, 'MGM became the first major Hollywood distributor to enter the "adults only" arena [of NC-17] with open eyes', and in exchange for complete artistic control, Verhoeven handed back 70 per cent of his $6-million fee, to be repaid if the film was a success (van Scheers, 1997, p. 268). As it turned out, *Showgirls* was a failure on both artistic and commercial levels. It became the first film to receive more nominations than there were categories in the 1995 Razzie awards.[16] Nominated thirteen times, it won seven.[17] Verhoeven, to his credit, then became the first director to turn up at the ceremony to collect his awards in person.

Showgirls proved to be no game-changer in terms of censorship and classification. While it did manage to lift, temporarily, the unofficial ban on the advertising of NC-17 category films, and while it was booked to open in almost 1,400 theatres nationwide, it ended up taking just over $20 million on a production budget of $38 million. The fact that this box-office return made

it the most successful NC-17 rated film ever released is an indicator of how
utterly the MPAA's efforts to change the rating system failed. In the end, it
did not take long for the NC-17 to follow a similar path to the X rating. With
press wary of advertising films branded with it, and with religious groups
uniting against the MPAA's initiative, and the Blockbuster video chain
refusing to stock any NC-17 films, the studios soon abandoned the rating in
the same way that they had dropped the X twenty years before.

Basic Instinct at the MPAA

No matter what Verhoeven had caught on film in terms of violence and,
especially, sex, there was always going to be a tight limit on what he was going
to be able to include in his final cut. Carolco had been adamant from the
beginning that they were not going to accept an NC-17-rated film: with a
budget of around $45 million to recoup, only an R-rated picture would do,
even if the company ended up having to take the film out of Verhoeven's
hands for the final edit. Verhoeven had already had some experience of
America's own particular form of censorship; what we might term, to
misquote Bruce Lee's character in *Enter the Dragon* (1973), 'the art of
censoring without censoring'. The MPAA had taken issue with every one of
his previous Hollywood films, and he knew that *Basic Instinct* would be even
more contentious than *Flesh + Blood* (1985), *RoboCop* and *Total Recall*;
RoboCop in particular had caused problems at the MPAA: its extreme and
protracted scenes of violence had to be re-edited eight times before it was
granted an R (Keesey and Duncan, 2005, p. 102). Knowing from the start that
he had to deliver an R-rated *Basic Instinct*, Verhoeven prepared accordingly,
making sure that he had enough coverage of the sex scenes, from different
angles and with different framings, so that he would be able to cut the movie
differently for the US and the European markets. 'Each time I felt there could
be a problem with the MPAA,' he told Laurent Bouzereau, 'I shot further
away, from another angle, with a different light or whatever, so I had a lot of

different possibilities.' Because of the care he took over coverage and additional footage, when the MPAA demanded cuts, Verhoeven was able to offer them 'another solution that was less explicit without changing the scene' (p. 203). The close comparison of the R-rated and the unrated (UR) versions below looks at these changes in detail.

Verhoeven has always been pragmatic about his position on censorship in the US context. In his interview with Laurent Bouzereau, he spoke at length about the different ways a film-maker could make sense of his or her position within the film industry, and the consequent conflicts of interest. 'This medium has two values, an artistic one and a commercial one. […] I think you kill the industry and good movies too if you consider film only as art.' For Verhoeven, the American approach is too commerce-driven, and in Europe, 'film is killed over there because of this art approach'; he concludes, 'You can't isolate art completely from its economic environment' (Bouzereau, 1994, pp. 207–8). At the same time, Verhoeven was quite happy to create mischief. He has spoken several times about how much he relishes the chance to challenge the limits of what is acceptable. The director recalled 'pushing it' in particular when shooting the oral-sex scenes between Nick and Catherine. Watching the videotape playback with Douglas, he says, the actor laughed, 'We won't get away with that.' Verhoeven quipped, 'Well, he was right. Not in the United States' (Rohrer, 1992).

By the end of January 1992, Verhoeven had assembled a first cut of the film for submission to the MPAA. Unsurprisingly, after two preliminary screenings the first submission in February was offered an NC-17 rating (Bonfante, 1992, p. 64). Despite Verhoeven's claim that the MPAA was urging him and the studio to release the film as an NC-17, Richard Heffner, head of CARA, recalls that the film was 'never going to [get] anything other than a hard R'. Heffner continues: 'But we would, as we did with all films, try to help these bastards enable us *responsibly* to give it an R rather than an NC-17' (cited in Sandler, 2007, p. 136). In the meantime, MPAA Head Jack Valenti apparently 'declared it was one of the most powerful movies he had ever seen' (Bouzereau, 1994, p. 187).

Whatever the detail of the wrangling behind closed doors, the publicity machine immediately swung into action. Douglas and Verhoeven suggested that the film company should accept the higher rating and allow the picture to be released uncut. Their reasoning was that the film had already generated enough hype to attract audiences, even with the near-taboo NC-17 tag. The insistence of director and star that the film's integrity should be valued above the commercial need for a lower classification was predictable, another cog in the myriad wheels of hype that spun around the movie from the beginning. Sandler notes that Jack Valenti 'hounded' Heffner over the rating of the movie, speculating that much of this had to do with Carolco's heavy investment in the film, and Michael Douglas's own personal financial stake in particular (Sandler, 2007, p. 230, n. 43). Of course, it was never really a genuine option: in an interview promoting the film in the UK, Verhoeven would admit that had the studio released an NC-17 version, 'we would have been reduced to some 200 cinemas across the States, whereas it is now on show in 1800' (Bergson, 1992, p. 4). Nevertheless, it worked as a reliable stimulus for further publicity (Banner, 1992, p. 17). Douglas made the most of the missing seconds from his scene with Sharon Stone in interviews promoting the movie, notably in an appearance on *The Tonight Show with Jay Leno* (Vaughn, 2006, p. 212).

Verhoeven eventually agreed to cut around forty-two seconds from the movie in order to achieve the R rating that the studio required. 'The task was to get as close to the impossible as possible,' he told one interviewer (Rohrer, 1992). The uncut version, however, would be released in Europe, where it would be given a rating ranging from 15 in Sweden to 18 in the UK and other territories. Once again, the marketing opportunity was too good to pass up, and, particularly where graphic sex in mainstream movies could still provoke sharp intakes of breath – as in the UK – the fact that the film was being shown uncut there no doubt excited and intrigued much of its target audience in these markets (see pp. 87–91). Indeed, Thomas Austin's research into the film's audience in the UK suggests that the ways in which the film was promoted, constructing it as an 'unmissable' event movie, was a motivating factor for many in their decision to go to see it (Austin, 2002, pp. 64–5).

Close Analysis: The Scenes Cut at CARA's Request

It is relatively easy to determine the detail of the cuts demanded by the MPAA by comparing the home-video 'Special Edition' R-rated US release of the film from 2001 against the 'Unrated Director's Cut' release that was issued simultaneously. The unrated release is also identical to the version screened in European cinemas, and has always been freely available on home video in Europe. Of course, it is impossible to know the details of what may have been cut from earlier versions assembled by Verhoeven before the European cut was finalised. For now, I will focus on the principles behind CARA's objections and Verhoeven's strategy for dealing with them. According to Verhoeven, the censorship decisions were to do with three specific aspects: nudity, sexual grinding, and explicit sex and violence (Sandler, 2007, p. 137), and sure enough the specific shots cut centre on precisely these moments. Verhoeven talks of a difference in running time of forty-two seconds between the European and the American cut of the film, with twenty-two seconds made up of actual cuts, and the rest comprising shots where different angles replaced the original footage. When the first cut was inevitably rejected by the MPAA, Verhoeven set to work re-editing the movie by replacing existing shots with different footage. Even so, a number of specific details of the sex scenes, as I will show, were cut entirely.

The Johnny Boz Scene Uncut

As the film's opening credits draw to a close, it appears the audience is viewing a room via an overhead shot. As the orchestral score settles on one sustained surge of strings, the camera tilts and we see that the angle has deceived us: at the top of the screen, two naked figures appear, lying on a bed and making love and we understand that we are watching them in a mirror, but our view of them is still horizontally inverted; it is not until the camera angle shifts again that it becomes clear we have been watching them in a mirror fixed to the ceiling above the bed.

The camera tracks around the edge of the bed: the woman, with long blonde hair hanging loose, is in the dominant position, straddling the man who groans as she moves her hips. Now the angle changes to a medium close-up of the woman's naked torso; however, we cannot see her face clearly, which is obscured by her hair. We switch to a close-up on the man's face, as the woman passes a manicured hand over his mouth. He sucks on her fingers. As he continues to moan, we hear her gasps, too, accompanied by a side view of her, a close-up on her head, shoulders and upper back (her face still obscured). The camera pans down past her breasts and settles on their two bodies, in medium close-up, as she continues to rock back and forth on top of him. A new angle, shot through the wrought iron at the head of the bed, gives an unmistakable impression of the bars of a cage.

The woman is now facing us directly, but we still cannot see her features. She takes the man's wrists and positions them behind his head, before tying them to the wrought iron of the bed frame with a white silk scarf. As she pulls it tight, punctuating the tug with a gasp, we see her through the bars once again; as she continues to tie him up, there are brief shots of the man straining upwards to kiss her nipple, and close-ups of the woman as she leans forward and over him. Now the music starts to build in volume and intensity, as do the moans and sighs of the lovers; the pace of the editing begins to pick up: close-ups of the man's face distorting in sexual pleasure; the woman from the waist up, her head swinging back and forth, then leaning back away from him as they move towards their climax. Just before orgasm, the camera, in a wider angle shot that shows both of them on the bed, moves behind the woman and swoops in, very rapidly, to focus on her right hand as she reaches for something beneath the covers. As the unsuspecting male continues to grunt and gasp, we see her grip a wooden-handled ice-pick. The camera angle is now back in front of the woman, waist up, as she arcs her body back, weapon poised, for a terrible blow.

A crash of cymbals on the rising soundtrack accompanies a close-up of the man's head and chest, as the ice-pick makes contact, the stabbing action aimed for the left side of the base of his neck (Figure 3). The woman

Figure 3: A frame included in both R-rated and UR cut.

tugs on the ice-pick, and as she withdraws it, gouts of blood appear, spurting across his shoulder. The film cuts back and forth between the woman, in close-up, as she continues to stab in the same scything, over-arm motion; the close-ups of the man include a shot of the ice-pick going into his face, just by the side of his nose, while his existing wounds spout blood (Figure 4). The woman's torso is now splashed with blood, too, and we see close-ups of her arm as she continues her frenzied attack, blood flying upwards. There are brief shots of the pick again entering the man's face, at one point appearing to get stuck, for a split-second, in the cartilage of his nose. Another wider angle from the bedside, which had previously shown the two bodies in the throes of passion, now reveals the terrible extent of the wounds the killer has inflicted across the victim's face and chest. The blood loss is copious. And this is the last we see of the crime: as the woman continues to stab, the film cuts abruptly to an exterior shot of a San Francisco street, with a car with a police-light visible on the dashboard, siren wailing, moving up

Figure 4: A frame cut from the R edit.

the hill toward us at considerable speed, before pulling in next to a line of cops and patrol cars.

Censorship of the Johnny Boz Scene

A comparison of the unrated (UR) with the R-rated (R) version of the scene reveals no differences between the two in the initial high-angle shot of the couple making love on the bed, but at the point where the UR version cuts to a medium close-up of the woman astride the man, the R edit remains in long shot for a couple of seconds longer. The closer angle makes the grinding more explicit and also gives the impression of extending the action. The Rating Board report notes that the sexual grinding had been 'reduced to "two revolving motions"' for the R version (Sandler, 2007, p. 137).

This aside, the most significant cuts are to the stabbing of Johnny Boz. In the R edit, there is only one impact shot: we see the ice-pick as it enters Boz's neck at the first stab. What remains of the footage of the killing in the R version is then very brief: we do not see the victim again after the first impact; we only see the killer, and mostly in medium close-up, since the R edit reduces the nudity significantly. A medium shot of the woman stabbing the man is replaced by a head-and-shoulder shot, and the length of the shot of the woman stabbing Boz repeatedly is reduced considerably. The final long shot of the woman astride Boz's body, still stabbing (Figure 5), has been cut entirely for the R version. In all, the killing is cut down by about four seconds, with the graphic shots of the stabs into the victim's nose excised entirely.

Although the amount of cut footage is not substantial, the impact on the scene as a whole is. The level of eroticism may not be significantly affected, but the murder itself is toned down considerably. The impact of the

Figure 5: This long shot of the murder of Johnny Boz
is missing from the R cut of the film.

uncut scene relies to a large extent on the unnerving shift from the graphic sex, inviting one particular set of responses from the audience, to the explicit violence, which (naturally) invokes a very different reaction: the R version shows only the ice-pick entering the man's neck from the first blow; the UR cut shows several more impact wounds, including a stab that goes through the left side of Boz's nose and out the other side. While both versions show blood splashing on the woman's breasts, the UR cut goes on to show, in long shot, the naked woman, still mounted, repeatedly stabbing her victim. The parallelism between the killing and the sex scene that has led up to this moment is underlined by the deployment of matching camera angles, and the actors' similar positions. The final shot before there is a cut to the next scene (Gus and Nick's car pulling up outside the murder scene) is of Johnny Boz and his killer, awash with blood: we see the woman stab Boz four more times, with Boz still moving beneath her, only this time in agony rather than ecstasy, an unnerving fusion of eroticism and extreme violence. The cut is abrupt: as we shift to the next scene, there is no sign of the ferocious assault ending, and the lack of a resolution – one might have expected a shot of the woman falling exhausted and spent on top of Boz – jars, intensifying the impact of the violence.

The Date-Rape Scene Uncut

The 'date-rape' sequence is in some ways the most problematic scene in the film. The opening murder is shockingly violent; the Nick/Catherine 'fuck-of-the-century' (FOTC) scene is the most explicitly erotic; but it is the scene between Beth and Nick that raises some of the most difficult questions about what Eszterhas wrote, and about how Verhoeven chose to shoot it. For those moved to protest against the movie, it was always the date-rape scene that was easiest to target, rather than the wider issues of the representation of the film's lesbian and bisexual characters (see pp. 30–1). Indeed, according to van Scheers's biography, Verhoeven's approach to the filming of the scene was conditioned by the director's impatience with politically correct protests: 'I thought, "If they want to take offence at something that much, then I'll give them something to take offence at!"' (van Scheers, 1997, p. 249).

It seems very feasible that Verhoeven decided to shoot the scene in the way he did as an act of provocation (in his DVD commentary, he claims that the scene was shot exactly as it was written in Eszterhas's screenplay). The original script frames the scene as something much closer to rape, with Beth protesting, 'Don't – please, Nick – […] Please don't – don't –'. This is followed by the direction, 'He puts his mouth to her shoulder, bites it – as they move down to the floor', at which point the scene ends.[18] The screenplay is in this way both less equivocal about Nick's act of violation, and more muted in what it suggests should be shot. The different assemblages of footage that make up the UR and the R versions of the scene are revealing about the sensitivity of the debate around the representation of rape on screen.

The encounter is initiated by Nick almost as soon as they have entered her apartment. Shrugging off his jacket and throwing it over a chair, he remains with his back to Beth. She approaches somewhat uncertainly and he turns; their eyes meet briefly and Beth looks to be about to break into a tentative smile when Nick makes a sudden, aggressive move: in an unmistakable attempt to establish immediate dominance, he pushes her against the wall, forcing her arms above her head. They kiss, and at this point it seems clear that what is happening is consensual. The camera pans down, tracking Nick's hand as it moves down Beth's body. The camera then pans back up as they continue to kiss and Nick fondles her breasts. They exchange a more confrontational look; Beth seems to be trying to figure out what Nick is thinking, but his face gives nothing away, and he tears open her blouse before pushing up her bra and ripping it open. Between each of these actions, he seems calmer and gentler, and the switch between aggression and what is almost tenderness is unsettling.

Without warning, Nick suddenly drags her across the room, slamming into the opposite wall, with Nick taking the impact as he turns Beth in his arms so that she ends up with her back to him, her arms pinned. He continues to fondle her, and there are a series of close-ups of them kissing, of Nick lifting her short skirt to expose her knickers and stockings, and medium shots that reveal Beth's exposed breasts. Again without warning, Nick pushes Beth forward and throws her over the back of a broad armchair. The angle switches from a long shot from behind, with Nick holding her bent over the back of the armchair, to a closer shot from in front, revealing Nick's near-crazed expression and Beth's pain and fear. There are also a couple of shots from the side, with a close-up on Beth's face. Beth emits cries of shock and protest. As he rips away her knickers, she struggles and continues to protest, but he keeps pushing her head down again onto the chairback, refusing to allow her to move out of position. We watch Nick as he unbuttons his trousers and drops them around his knees and as he forces himself upon Beth. Nick's aggressive expression remains fixed as he thrusts into her from behind,[19] and we also see him tear the blouse down off Beth's left shoulder, the latter caught in medium close-up from the camera in front of them. Beth says 'no' once more and then Nick enters her, and it is at this point that Beth seems to stop struggling. There are, however, no signs of pleasure. Nick soon climaxes, and there is some kissing, with Nick still leaning over her shoulder, before the scene cuts to the aftermath.

Censorship of the Date-Rape Scene

In his interview with Laurent Bouzereau Verhoeven spoke at some length about the date-rape scene, noting that the US version ended up being about twenty seconds shorter than the European cut, and that each version also used different shots (in the same way that the FOTC scene was assembled differently for the different markets). 'In the American version,' he notes, 'it's kind of indicated, but then it's over. In the European version, it really hits it several times, WOW! WOW! WOW!' (Bouzereau, 1994, p. 203).

The R version of the sex scene between Nick and Beth is uncut up to the point when we see him throw her over the back of the armchair. From

Figure 6: Shot missing from the R cut of the film.

this point, the UR version runs for thirty-seven seconds, with the R cut
clocking in at a fraction over half that length. We still see the long shot from
behind when Nick removes Beth's underwear, but this shot is much shorter
in the R version, and most of the R scene uses footage shot from in front
of the couple. The R cut does not show Nick pulling his trousers down or
entering her (see Figure 6). There is also much less thrusting. In fact, due to
the way the scene is cut, it looks as if Nick climaxes as soon as he thrusts into
her (an action we only see from the camera angle in front of the couple, not
behind). More significantly, in the R version, there are only muffled noises of
protest to be heard from Beth. In the longer UR cut, we clearly hear Beth say:
'Nick … stop … no … no … please … no … no', and there are several more,
inarticulate cries as she struggles to resist. Furthermore, the UR cut shows
Nick slamming Beth's head down against the chairback not once but twice
more as she struggles, further emphasising his brutality: this footage is
missing from the R version.

Without a doubt, the sequence raises the familiar spectre of the male rape myth: the idea that a woman may, while insisting 'no', really mean 'yes'. In the aftermath, we find Dan and Beth lying together, somewhat awkwardly. The conversation that follows, with Beth struggling to understand the aggression in his lovemaking ('You've never been like that before'), reveals the depth of her unhappiness:

> Beth: You weren't making love to me.
> Nick: Who was I making love to?
> Beth: You weren't making love.

Contentiously, Bouzereau suggests in his interview with Verhoeven that, 'In the European version, it's more obvious she's consenting', and he asks whether Verhoeven agrees with the description of the encounter as a 'date rape' (Bouzereau, 1994, p. 203). 'A date-rape would really be that she is raped and that at no moment is there any consent,' Verhoeven replies, and although he is under no illusion that what Nick does in this scene is morally wrong, he prevaricates over the precision of the 'date-rape' term. 'There is consent and there are moments when you feel it's going too far, and then she consents anyhow for whatever reason' (p. 203), he muses, adding, 'he pushes her in to [sic] a situation that ultimately I don't know if she enjoys it, but she seems to accept it to a certain degree' (p. 204). His remarks on the DVD commentary express similar sentiments: 'Of course it is close to a date rape. And it goes up and down between she [sic] wanting it and basically perhaps being brutalised. … You're not sure exactly what the balance is here. Is it something she likes…?' In the interview with Bouzereau, Verhoeven muses that 'when she invites him [to her apartment] she wants to fuck … . The question is that the way she fucks is not exactly the way that she imagined she would be fucked' (p. 204).

Verhoeven's phrasing of his perspective on the scene is revealing. Even taking account of the fact that English is not his first language, and acknowledging the format of the discourse – presumably a transcript of a face-to-face interview – the slip between the active ('she fucks') and the passive voice ('she would be fucked') is significant. Bouzereau suggests that Beth attempts to 'seduce' Nick by inviting him back to her apartment, but at no point does the exchange between them in the bar, or what passes between them in dialogue or non-verbal communication back at the apartment, suggest that she is in control of what is happening. Bouzereau suggests that, 'I felt […] that she was trying to seduce him by inviting him over to her apartment in the first place' (p. 204), but in fact, it is Nick who says to Beth, 'Do you want to get out of here?' and she agrees. The film then cuts to them arriving at Beth's apartment. The UR release of the film makes Beth's initial attempt to resist Nick's sexual assault unequivocal. This is expressed via the number of times she protests – at least half a dozen – and the force with which Nick holds her down, which is also clearer in the UR cut. Even less equivocal are the two times we see Nick slam her head against the top of the chair. It would be difficult to make a convincing case for the encounter as 'aggressive sex', as Douglas did in the interview quoted above (see p. 37).

Camille Paglia, in her commentary track on the DVD, justifies the scene from a different perspective, but with a similar intent. The brutality of the sexual encounter is 'in keeping with the theme of *Basic Instinct*', she argues. She believes that Beth seems to 'half-respond' to Nick's initiative. However, 'Nick treats her brutally', forcing sex on her from behind, and Paglia concludes that 'the scene does seem to become a rape'. At the same time, Paglia's point of view is not very far removed from Douglas's, and she is characteristically scathing about how the film would have to be 'sanitised' if it were to be made today in the 'current climate': the rape scene would have to conclude, she suggests, with Nick locked in the bathroom weeping with remorse after his assault on Beth. Once again, we return to the contested territory of political correctness. However, the rhetorical strategies are markedly different: while Douglas tries to justify the scene by choosing to define it as 'aggressive sex' rather than sexual assault, Paglia *is* prepared to frame the scene as a rape, but suggests that to complain about the film's representation of a date rape is simple-minded, over-sensitive and overly politically correct.

The FOTC Scene Uncut

From sex and violence, to sexual violence, to straightforward sex: the so-called fuck-of-the-century (FOTC) scene, the long love scene between Nick and Catherine, would be the sequence most heavily cited as problematic for CARA. The scene exemplifies the most ground-breaking aspect of the film as far as its portrayal of sex is concerned; Hollywood had never seen anything this explicit in a mainstream movie. The Rating Board, usually far more disturbed by sex than by violence, believed quite specific lines had been crossed relating to the regulation of representations of sexual activity. Once again, Verhoeven's technique of shooting footage from a number of different angles would enable him to meet CARA's requirements without drastically shortening the scene.

The scene begins with a close-up of Catherine and Nick kissing as he lays her down on the bed. It then cuts to a long shot, with the couple on the bed at the right-hand side of the frame. As Nick moves to a kneeling position to remove his sweater, we switch to a medium close-up on him, then a medium shot of Catherine, naked, lying on the bed. Nick comes into frame as he moves back down on top of her, and he kisses and fondles her breasts. There is a cut to Catherine in close-up as Nick disappears from the frame, kissing down her body. The focus is on Catherine's reaction, before a cut to a medium long shot that shows Nick kissing just above her pubic area, as Catherine runs her hands over her breasts. A sequence of shots follows showing Nick in close-up, raising his head from between her legs, a shot of Catherine's face and breasts from Nick's point of view, then a medium long shot as Nick lifts her leg over his shoulder and prepares to go down on her. The sequence then cuts back to a medium close-up of Catherine from Nick's position, followed by a shot from Catherine's POV of Nick giving her oral sex, cutting back to Catherine as she reaches orgasm.

There is a time ellipsis in the next cut, which offers a new angle from a camera positioned behind the head of the bed, shooting through the bars.[20] The camera pans up to a shot of Catherine astride Nick, who is kissing her breasts. Cut to a close-up of them kissing, to a tracking shot from the head of the bed to the side, and another close-up of Catherine kissing Nick's chest. An angle above and slightly to the side captures them in medium shot, as Catherine moves down Nick's body. The camera then pans and tilts up towards the mirror, and we see their reflections in long shot, with Catherine performing fellatio. The camera cuts to Nick's reaction from Catherine's POV, before Catherine moves back up to kiss Nick in close-up. The overhead long shot from the mirror's perspective is repeated as Catherine lies on top of Nick, and they then roll over.

The next shot is another medium close-up in side view of Nick on top of Catherine as he presumably enters her, and the next sequence switches from this shot, to close-ups of Nick's face, and to Catherine's face, as the orchestral score builds. As they move towards orgasm, the sequence cuts to the angle from behind the head of the bed, with Catherine gripping the bars, back to a close-up on her face and Nick kissing her neck. Their cries become increasingly frantic, and there is a shot from above as Catherine digs her nails into his back, drawing long, red scratches. We cut to a close-up on Nick rising away from her as he climaxes, in ecstasy and pain, followed by a close-up on Catherine's face.

They roll over (again seen through the bars), and we switch to a shot from the side of the bed in medium close-up as Catherine straddles Nick. Forcing his arms back behind his head, she whispers, 'Shh …' until he stops struggling against her, and the film cuts from close-ups of their faces to a side view. As Catherine pulls a white silk scarf from under the pillow beneath Nick's head, the camera lingers on Nick's shocked expression, switching from him to a medium close-up of Catherine smiling as she plays with the silk. The theme from the opening scene returns as she ties his wrists to the bars of the bedhead, and the camera angles switch from the shot through the bars, to a side view in medium shot. Having tied him up, Catherine begins to grind on top of Nick, as the orchestral score builds again in a repeat of the earlier 'climax sequence'. From a close-up of Catherine's face, the sequence cuts to a long shot of her bucking on top of him, then leaning back away from him, cutting to a medium close-up on Catherine. In a repeat of the shot from the Boz sequence, there is a close-up of her hand reaching behind her, next to Nick's foot, sliding beneath the cover. There is a fleeting close-up of Nick's grimacing face which cuts to a shot from behind the bedhead of Catherine arching back, then swooping and dropping on top of Nick. The music reaches its climax and falls away with Catherine's back and shoulder obscuring Nick's face. The camera behind the bed shoots Catherine untying the scarf; cut to a close-up of Nick panting, relieved, and a long shot of Catherine still astride Nick. He sits up and leans forward and they embrace, both out of breath, before we cut to Catherine's face, enigmatic, as he buries his head in her chest. The final cut is another time ellipsis, and a long shot with the two of them lying in bed together, partially under the covers.

Censorship of the FOTC Scene

As Verhoeven points out on his commentary track, it is 'nearly impossible' to have a sex scene run for as long as this one does – four minutes – without it becoming 'irritating, embarrassing or pornographic'. (Verhoeven refers to the scene being nearly three minutes long – uncut, it is in fact almost four). If the scene does work – and some critics were scathing about it – it is because of the way in which narrative takes precedence and in this sense it is not primarily a love scene, but a tense instalment in the unfolding of the story. The scene is of course deliberately very reminiscent of the opening Johnny Boz scene, and the theme is underlined by the return of the same musical score, and such techniques as the camera tilt above the bed, the use of the silk scarf, and some repeated actions and camera angles replicated from the Boz scene.

In the R version, a fleeting side-view glimpse of Nick's penis, in the longshot of the two of them on the bed, seems to have been digitally removed. A close-up of Catherine's face as she reacts to Nick going down on her has been removed, and as Nick performs oral sex, we no longer see Catherine running her hands over her breasts in medium shot (Figure 7). Verhoeven has

Figure 7: A shot missing from the R edit.

replaced this with a long shot from the same angle as the beginning of the scene, with Catherine spreading her arms back above her head. The medium shot in the UR version showing Nick between Catherine's legs and kissing the inside of her thigh is replaced by a close-up of Nick's face and Catherine's leg: this removes one shot of Catherine's naked body from the sequence. The frames in which Nick performs oral sex in close-up have been excised entirely, although we still see Catherine's face as she climaxes, and the implied action is unmistakable.

As the sequence shifts to a camera panning up from behind the head of the bed, a shot of Catherine above Nick, and Nick kissing her breasts, is altered in the R version, which instead includes a brief, less explicit shot, and then cuts and remains on a close-up of the two of them kissing. A medium shot which reveals Catherine's naked body as she kisses Nick's chest is missing; instead, the camera remains on her in close-up. The sequence seen in the ceiling mirror (Figure 8) is drastically shortened in the R edit: the shot is

Figure 8: A shot in the mirror of fellatio is much shorter in the R edit.

fleeting, perhaps two and a half seconds shorter than the UR version. When the
sequence cuts back to Nick in close-up, this shot is slightly longer, but Nick's
groan has been edited out. As they roll over, the uncut film cuts back to the
mirrored ceiling, and we see their naked bodies in long shot from above. The R
version omits this entirely (a couple of seconds total), but the shot that replaces
it – the two of them rolling over in bed to leave Nick on top – is longer and
slightly tighter. Interestingly, it reveals much more evidently some pink scratches
on Nick's back: this probably makes more obvious a continuity error that is
easier to miss in the UR cut (Catherine has not yet scraped her fingernails across
his back, and the marks are not visible at the point where Catherine climaxes).
This part of the scene is shorter than the UR cut. However, it is worth noting
that the R version includes a brief side-view medium shot of Catherine
underneath Nick, revealing her breasts, that is not part of the sequence in the
UR version. Finally, a brief long shot of Catherine straddling Nick and bucking
has been removed (Figure 9) – the camera instead lingers slightly longer on a

Figure 9: A shot missing from the R edit.

medium close-up – and although this part of the scene is the same length in the two versions, there is again the impression of slightly less nudity.

Sandler identifies the key criteria used by the Rating Board in determining whether or not a film can be granted an R certificate. These include 'full body shots of fornication; prolonged sexual thrusting or grinding; onscreen imagery of anal sex or oral sex, and the visibility of pubic hair or the penis during a sexual act' (Sandler, 2007, p. 139). It is also interesting to note that the unabashed representations of oral sex – both fellatio and cunnilingus – had to be considerably reduced, either by shortening the offending sequence or providing less detail, or both. Furthermore, while the sight and sound of Catherine's orgasm was acceptable, the same did not apply to Nick, whose groan following the shot of Catherine performing fellatio was edited out.

It is worth mentioning in passing that a third version of the film was assembled for network TV broadcast in the US, and Laurent Bouzereau describes this version in some detail in his chapter about the film. The changes include further cuts to Boz's murder, removing all nudity and further trimming the stabbing, and no full frontal male nudity at the crime scene. The offending 'flash' sequence was removed from the interrogation scene. All nudity was removed from the date-rape scene, and there are clearly articulated 'no's from Beth that are missing from the US R version. The FOTC scene had all frontal nudity removed, as did Nick and Catherine's second love scene and the final scene (these scenes generally had medium and long shots replaced with close-ups of the couple kissing). There were major cuts to Gus's death scene, and Bouzereau also painstakingly tracks all the dialogue changes, which replaced all the explicit language with more acceptable euphemisms (Bouzereau, 1994, pp. 191–7). These changes are not, in the end, very interesting in themselves. US network television has always been notoriously squeamish about sex, bad language and, to a lesser extent, violence. However, the TV version is interesting for the fact that Verhoeven apparently added Beth's protests during the date-rape scene 'to convey the fact that Beth is not entirely consenting' (Bouzereau, 1994, p. 193), providing another twist on the debate about the scene, and whether it does or does not tend to endorse the male rape myth.

Basic Instinct at the BBFC

While *Basic Instinct* endured a troubled passage through the corridors of the MPAA, it fared rather better in the UK, where the registration form at the BBFC, dated 13 March 1992, noted the length of the footage (11,522 feet and 4 frames, 128 minutes and 1 second) and a straightforward 'Pass "18" no cuts'.[21] Although no edits were demanded by the BBFC, the reports are nevertheless interesting for what they reveal about the examiners' approach to the classification process, and about the potential pressure points with regard to sex, violence and sexual violence.

The *BBFC Annual Report for 1992* suggests that the Board was at this time more or less resigned to sequences of graphic violence in mainstream film: 'The trouble is that screen violence is found now not just in a few high-profile titles, but as a staple in far too many big-budget movies', the *Report* remarks, in decidedly regretful tones (BBFC, 1993, p. 12). *Basic Instinct* is not name-checked in the discussion; *Terminator 2* (1992), *Lethal Weapon 2* (1989), Kathryn Bigelow's surf-cop movie *Point Break* (1992) and the Steven Seagal vehicle *Under Siege* (1991) are cited as examples of thrillers with high levels of graphic violence. The *Report* contrasts these films with those that, it claimed, 'took violence seriously', citing 'independent and low-budget' (and generally critically acclaimed) films such as *Boyz n the Hood* (1991) and *American Me* (1992), described as 'an antidote to the shoot-em-up thrillers' which had 'cheapened' issues such as inner-city violence. The *Report* also cites *Reservoir Dogs* and *Romper Stomper* (both 1992) as two movies that 'treated violence as the ugly, self-destructive thing it is'. In a rather mind-boggling twist, it goes on to compare Tarantino's film's ending, which leaves the scene 'littered with corpses' with the final tableau in *Hamlet. Reservoir Dogs* and *Romper Stomper* (a film about Nazi skinheads in Melbourne) were both seen as 'moral tale[s] about the breakdown of morality' (BBFC, 1993, p. 11).

In considering the film's sexual content, again, the Board recognised that, by the beginning of the 1990s, the boundaries of taste had shifted considerably. The 1992 *Report* suggests, 'There has been a slow but perceptible liberalisation in Britain during the eighties, particularly in mainstream films, as it became clear that the public are less concerned about media sex than media violence' (BBFC, 1993, p. 15). In this context, while the sex scenes in *Basic Instinct* remained some of the strongest submitted in a mainstream film, they were hardly likely to itch the examiners' scissor fingers. Having said that, it is worth noting that one of the two reports does mention a single fleeting glimpse of male nudity, featured in the film's second scene, as the forensic team and the investigators survey the corpse of Johnny Boz. The examiner describes the sequence: '[T]he camera coldly scanning the victim who is pooled in blood which has run down over his groin and genitals', and remarks, 'Would we permit this shot if the victim were female? I doubt it!'

There are two reports on file, one by a male examiner whom I will refer to as GL and one by a female examiner, whom I will refer to as CT. GL flags up 'sex, sexual violence and splatter' as classification issues and describes the movie as 'A gripping piece of hokum which bounces the eyeballs from the very start with a scorching sex scene followed by a brutal bloody ice-pick slaying of the man by the woman astride him'. It is interesting to note that GL attributes the film's 'edge of one's seat' quality to the opening scene, which he describes as 'extraordinarily powerful and in the end bloodily violent' and as 'a sequence set up to be as erotically effective as the director can manage'. GL notes the potentially problematic scenes and details the amount of nudity and the sexual acts represented throughout; he notes that the FOTC scene 'begins with the opening of Reel 5 and goes on for 4 mins 20 secs in which masked cunnilingus, fellatio, bondage of the male, and energetic riding to implied orgasm all occur'; CT describes the same scene as 'astonishingly erotic' and adds that it 'thankfully stayed this side of cutting since it moved from activity to activity (including powerfully impressive cunnilingus), angle to angle without staying long enough to build graphic details of the sex'. CT makes a point in terms of case history, comparing *Basic Instinct*'s opening sequence to the opening killing of *Jagged Edge*, which she believes the BBFC had cut on film and video.[22] She notes that,

> Since the victim here is a man and thus a powerful victim, the sight of him tied stabbed and naked in the next scene rang none of the warning bells that would have sounded if he had been a powerless woman victim.

In her examiner's report, CT remarks that, 'As a combination of sex, violence and bondage, this [opening scene] has it all but was utterly integral to the rest of the film in the way of scene and character setting.' There are references in GL's report to other scenes featuring nudity (Nick watching Catherine dress before taking her to the precinct for questioning; the interrogation scene) and he concludes that, 'These levels of voyeurism – both for the characters in the movie, and the audience who is asked unashamedly to take pleasure in the perusal of nudity and the watching of sex – very much militates for our "18".' The references in the film to drug use (Catherine's line, 'Have you ever fucked on cocaine, Nick?' and the mention that traces of the same drug were found on the lips and penis of Johnny Boz) constitute another BBFC red flag, but were not deemed problematic; as GL wryly comments, 'Since the result seems to be that you get stabbed with an ice pick it might well be said to be aversive in effect.' CT notes of the drug use that it is acceptable because it is 'calculated to show sleaze and decadence rather than excitement and pleasure'. The stabbings of Johnny Boz and Gus – both scenes cut by the MPAA – were noted by CT as 'unquestionably "18" on both qualitative and quantitative grounds – many stabs, blood spurting and gushing, but within general bounds for category'.

Considering the sex scene between Beth and Nick, GL details the angle at which it is filmed: 'buttocks to camera – though in long shot. He then penetrates her from behind, her cried out comment being "Fuck me – no!" which could, I guess, imply buggery, but nothing is explicit here.' CT is less concerned about explicit detail, but her report notes how closely the scene skirts the dangerous territory of the endorsement of sexual violence: Nick's assault on Beth 'initially seems to be something she doesn't welcome', she notes, 'But turns seamlessly into excitement for her, too, so the scene becomes less one of sexual violence, more one of passion illuminated briefly by fear – one of the movies [sic] themes.' The first half of this sentence seems to raise the very fraught issue of the male rape myth that a woman might say 'no' but really mean 'yes', discussed above (see pp. 58–63). This had become a familiar bugbear for the BBFC, particularly under the directorship of James Ferman (1975–99). However, in this particular case, the examiner moves swiftly past the initial red flag ('something she doesn't welcome') to deploy an aesthetic judgment on the film, with a reference to one of its 'themes'. With the sexual violence glossed instead as 'passion illuminated by fear', the potential problem is apparently obviated.

CT's commentary on the aesthetics of the film extends to the opening scene which, though intense ('this has it all'), she believes, is 'utterly integral to the rest of the film in the way of scene and character setting'. Effectively, the argument is the familiar one that the sexual violence is 'justified' by its context and consequently escapes the charge of gratuitousness. Her concluding comment is that the film is 'a must for an evening screening'. In sum, the reports could scarcely have been more glowing (and might have provided good copy for the distributor's marketing department, had they not been confidential!).

The Board's position on the film is underlined by an exchange of letters between the Deputy Director and a member of the public who had complained about what she described as 'a totally perverted film', making a familiar causal connection between representations of sex and violence and a decline in moral standards in society: 'I can wholeheartedly understand some of the reasons behind the sexual behavioural problems that are occurring in society if this is an example of the standard of films being portrayed today' (sic).[23] The Board's response was straightforward: 'The scenes of violence and sex seemed to us to be a part of the whole and not exploited and were therefore justified in context'. The letter also reminds the correspondent that the film had been passed at 18, for adults only.[24] A letter from another member of the public declared, 'Never in my whole life (60 years) have I seen and heard such <u>FILTH!</u> .... It was sickening and utterly DISGUSTING!' [emphasis in the original]. It continues:

> I now honestly believe that this type of film is the cause of so much rape and sex attacks, I should imagine men & young boys get hyped up to such an extent that any female – young or old is vulnerable to such an attack.

The letter also complains about the depiction of drugs 'to experiment with'. Once again, the tactful reply conceded that 'due to its explicit visuals of violence and sex it was felt proper that distribution should be restricted to adults who might then come to their own conclusions upon the worth of the work', notes that the characters in the film are 'ambivalent' about the drug abuse, and concludes by reminding the complainant that 'no other country has found it necessary to ban this film from viewing by an adult audience'.[25]

Media Effects?

Although the uncut version of *Basic Instinct* was screened across Europe
without raising any censors' eyebrows, two quirky footnotes to the history of
the film's censorship are worthy of note. The first comes courtesy of the mayor
of a small town in southwest France, Les Herbiers, who made the decision
to ban the film from local cinemas. 'Mayor Jeanne Briand claimed the film
"would release a sickness" in the community,' according to one report, which
also noted that she admitted that she had not seen it, but read about it in a
Christian magazine. Culture Minister Jack Lang asked her to reconsider 'In
the name of all those for whom freedom of creation remains a fundamental
value', but she refused to back down, citing a number of letters from
sympathisers and mayors 'who are thinking of doing the same thing', although
there are no reports of any of them following suit (*Independent*, 1992, p. 16).

The second footnote relates to the BBFC's role in the regulation of
home video in the UK, which began in the mid-1980s. The home-video
revolution had led to a rising sense of panic, in particular among the editorials
and news reports of the right-wing press, about the fact that material
unsuitable for children was available to them in the form of videos with
graphic sexual and violent content.[26] A working party was set up between
the British Videogram Association (the video distributors' organisation)
and the BBFC, working towards the establishment of a classification system
for home-video releases, established in 1984 under the terms of the Video
Recordings Act. An amendment followed ten years later, requiring the Board
to have 'special regard to the likelihood of works being viewed in the home'
and to 'any harm to those likely to view a video' and to 'any harm to society
through the behaviour of those viewers afterwards' (BBFC, 2000, p. 4). The
amendment had come about as a result of the press furore over the murder of
James Bulger, a two-year-old boy abducted, tortured and killed by two ten-
year-olds in Liverpool in 1993, and suggestions that the murderers, Robert
Thompson and Jon Venables, had been influenced by exposure to violent
media. Although there was not, as Julian Petley points out, one shred of

evidence of such a link, the momentum behind the press campaign had become unstoppable, and the amendment passed into law ten years after the original VRA had been established (see Petley, 2011, pp. 83–4, 87–97).

With this as context, I will turn to a number of reports in the UK press in August 1995 that relayed a bizarre story from Portsmouth Crown Court. A 'depressed housewife' named Vanessa Ballantyne (Pierce, 1995, p. 3) had spent the evening watching *Basic Instinct* on video, then took a knife from her kitchen (presumably in the absence of an ice-pick), went out to a night-club, where she picked up a man, led him down an alley and, with the words, 'I've got something for you,' proceeded to attack him with the knife. According to prosecutor Susan Holmes, '"She said the film had suggested to her that it would be a good idea to stab a man and left home that evening with that intent"' (Pierce, 1995, p. 3). The reports also noted that Ballantyne had been suffering from psychotic depression at the time of the attack. The victim was treated for a stomach wound in hospital and the perpetrator gave herself up to police a week later.

It is no surprise that the press reports made explicit the link between the incident and *Basic Instinct.* The *Guardian* ran with the headline, 'Housewife "acted out film stabbing"' (Knewstubb, 1995), while the *Daily Mail* announced 'Video led to knife attack' (*Daily Mail,* 1995, p. 33). *The Times* claimed, highly contentiously, that, 'The film was heavily criticised because of its violent content' (Pierce, 1995, p. 3). As we have seen, in the US, there was more concern over the graphic sex and nudity than there was over the violence, and in the UK the BBFC staff had lost no sleep whatsoever over a more complete version. Furthermore, as we shall see in Part 4, the press attention would be generated largely by the arguments over the representations of bisexuality rather than excessive violence. And if the film would end up being 'heavily criticised' by film critics, then 'violent content' would emerge fairly low on the priority list.

✖ PART 4

REVIEWING *BASIC INSTINCT*

Opening and Reception

Basic Instinct opened in the US on 20 March 1992 on around 1,500 screens, taking over $15 million in its opening weekend, and doubling the takings of the second-highest-grossing film that week, the comedy *Wayne's World* (*Orlando Sentinel*, 1992). *Basic Instinct* would end up charting ninth in the Top Ten box-office hits of the year. It was also the fourth-highest R-rated picture of the year, behind three star-powered vehicles, Mel Gibson in *Lethal Weapon 3*, Tom Cruise in *A Few Good Men* and Kevin Costner and Whitney Houston in *The Bodyguard*. It was clear that Carolco had banked on *Basic Instinct* to achieve a level of success that would help ease its ongoing financial difficulties (Weinraub, 1992): at the beginning of 1992, in the context of a severe economic recession, it was reported to be struggling with $171 million of debt (Greig, 1992, p. 13). Within a few weeks, the Los Angeles riots, which had been sparked by the acquittal of police officers charged with assaulting Rodney King, would impact severely on cinema attendance. With LA audiences accounting for up to 5 per cent of the cinemagoing audience in the US, a citywide curfew in the wake of the riots had a significant impact over a period of several weeks (*Vindicator*, 1992). Nevertheless, *Basic Instinct* remained at number one in the chart for four of the five weeks following its opening weekend (*Pittsburgh Press*, 1992), even if its continued chart-topping success was in part 'mostly for want of competition', as one report noted: the film returned to the top spot in its eighth week, but with a 'relatively modest' $4 million gross (*Entertainment Weekly*, 1992, p. 56).

The gay and lesbian activists, having failed to influence either the pre-production or shooting stages of the making of the film, took their protests to what they saw as the next level. 'We know that they went ahead without doing what we asked for,' Annette Gaudino of Queer Nation told the *Los Angeles*

Times. 'So now we're going to do what we have to do to keep the public away from this film' (Marx, 1992). However, although the studio and theatres braced themselves for widespread attempts to disrupt opening engagements around the country, there was nothing on the scale of the protests during shooting. Predictably, San Francisco saw the liveliest action. Hundreds of protesters gathered on the sidewalks outside the Metro Theatre on Union Street, waving placards and banners, many of them wearing T-shirts with the legend 'Catherine Did It!' in an attempt to give away the ending of the movie to the cinemagoers (the slogan was also used as the name for a specific group of activists, hailing from the San Francisco chapter of Queer Nation). The same T-shirts declared, 'Ice-pick wielding bisexual fag-dyke – do not agitate' on the back (Ellicott, 1992, p. 1). Once again, the protests achieved high-profile media exposure, even featuring in reports in the *Wall Street Journal* and in TV reports for *Good Morning America* and *USA Today* (Kauffman, 1992, p. 36). Journalists found themselves in an awkward position as they reported on the events, having to edit out the name from the 'Catherine Did It!' slogan, and masking it in photographs, in order to avoid broadcasting the film's ending to readers and viewers. Eszterhas, despite his earlier support for the activists, was angered by the strategy of revealing the film's ending to queuing audiences. 'If moviegoers decide to pay for a movie ticket', he said, 'then no one has the right to waste that money for them' (Kauffman, 1992, p. 36).

In the wake of a campaign by the studio and others opposed to the disruptions which spotlit the issue of free speech, the protesters were careful in the way they articulated their motives and their aims. Lyons quotes a piece of literature produced by a coalition of pressure groups in New York which is representative of the tone adopted at this stage of the campaign: wary of being accused of censorship again, the flyer pointed out to the audience that the movie 'could do us harm, by reinforcing ignorance about homosexuality, and by providing an excuse for an escalating number of assaults on women, lesbians, bisexuals, and gay men'. It went on to reassure its reader that the intention was not to question her right to see the movie, but suggested, 'We would like you to ask yourself whether you support the messages Hollywood sends out' (Lyons, 1997, p. 141). A spokesperson for Catherine Did It! attempted to clarify their stance on freedom of expression: 'Please do not confuse us with those people who censor artists … . Our goal is to bring to your attention Hollywood's consistently defamatory treatment of gays and lesbians' (Lyons, 1997, pp. 135–6). 'This movie links up sex and violence in an irresponsible way,' GLAAD co-leader Jehan Agrama protested. She continued: 'We are not asking people to boycott this movie. We are not calling for censorship. We just want to educate people' (Harris and Corwin, 1992).

If, as one activist claimed, the aim was 'to destroy the first weekend's box-office grosses',[27] the protests were a failure. However, the party line was held relatively consistently: the pressure groups expressed a degree of qualified contentment that they had made significant advances in raising awareness of the issues. So, in a phone interview with Charles Lyons on the eve of the film's premiere, GLAAD representative Elle Carten reflected that the campaign had been 'a success because we have gotten the word out'; she believed they were 'changing consciousness around issues'. She also ventured that 'I don't think anyone could go out and make a movie like this again or spend three million dollars in optioning a script like this' (Lyons, 1997, p. 137). Annette Gaudino of Queer Nation reckoned, 'This movie has the largest publicity machine on the planet and we're riding that machine' (Ellicott, 1992, p. 1). On the other hand, several journalists and commentators noted the bitter irony of the campaigners' impact on the reception of the film: it was clear to many that the protests had done little but hype the movie even further. One 'Tri-Star insider' gloated that 'the protests are worth millions … . You couldn't buy the advertising' (Banner, 1992, p. 17).

As noted already (see pp. 29–31), the protests against *Basic Instinct* can be seen as part of a wider assault on the Hollywood establishment by gay and lesbian pressure groups at this time. Both *JFK*, Oliver Stone's paranoid version of the Kennedy assassination, and *The Silence of the Lambs* had been targeted, the former for the depiction of a group of conspirators as gay, the latter for its representation of the confused sexuality of the serial killer being pursued by Clarice Starling (Jodie Foster).[28] Oliver Stone's film had received eight

Academy Award nominations (winning two), and *The Silence of the Lambs* had won five awards, including Best Picture. There were even accusations of a 'conspiracy', with complaints that *Paris Is Burning* (1990, a documentary about transvestites in Harlem) and *Truth or Dare* (1991), the Madonna tour film, had been overlooked for Oscar nominations (Ellicott, 1992, p.1).[29] Plans were announced to picket the Academy Awards ceremony in March 'to make the point that *Basic Instinct*, *JFK* and *The Silence of the Lambs* give an unflattering portrait of homosexuals' (Tran, 1992, p. 6).[30]

A number of commentators continued to support the action: the reviewer for *Gay Times* felt that the protests were effective in raising awareness of the issues (*Gay Times*, 1992, p. 69). Some activists and writers had rather more mixed feelings, however. Speaking to the *Sun-Times*, lesbian writer B. Ruby Rich, Visiting Professor at Berkeley University, felt that 'Responding to Hollywood product and judging its positive and negative values is a doomed venture […]. What's important [are] the gay and lesbian films that aren't getting any attention.' She cited Derek Jarman's film adaptation of Christopher Marlowe's play about the homosexual king Edward II, opening in New York at that time, as an example. 'Those who put all their emotion and energy into protesting "Basic Instinct" instead of promoting "Edward II" deserve what they get,' she remarked (Sachs, 1992, p. 1). Sachs's article usefully explores the complexities of the debates arising out of the attempts to censor *Basic Instinct* from the grassroots. He suggests that a recent spate of films about gays and lesbians, including *My Own Private Idaho* (1991), *Young Soul Rebels* (1991), *Paris Is Burning*, *Poison* (1991) and *Longtime Companion*, might be indicative of a sea change in Hollywood. He also raises the spectre of political correctness 'contributing to the bloodletting of color and risk from movies and other forms of popular culture' and the extent to which the 'liberal-minded souls all too eerily resembled the right-wingers who launched virulent, pre-emptive attacks' on Martin Scorsese's *The Last Temptation of Christ* (1988), Robert Mapplethorpe's photographic exhibitions and 'any number of works of homosexual art' (Sachs, 1992, p. 1).

Two writers for the *Village Voice*, which had previously carried a
dismissive review of the film by J. Hoberman (1992) as well as an explicit
attack on the film's supposed homophobia by Richard Goldstein (1992), were
inclined to wonder what all the fuss had been about. C. Carr declared she had
'got a kick out of the movie' and Amy Taubin suggested that, had some of the
(mostly male) critics who had attacked the film 'consulted some women […]
they might have discovered that a lot of us (lesbians, bis, and straights)
thought it was a gas to see a woman on the screen in a powerful enough
position to kill and let it all hang out and *not* be punished in the end' (cited
in Appiah, 1993, p. 86). A TV producer working on a programme about
Hollywood homophobia, Claire Beavan, concurred: 'For me, a cute dyke with
two Ferraris who kills men is a positive image,' she quipped (Picardie, 1992,
p. 36). Meanwhile, arguing from a more neutral standpoint, L. A. Kauffman,
for the monthly publication *Progressive*, wondered what 'positive role models'
were, and who might be fit to define them. 'Bring together any five people
who share an identity to talk about what representations of themselves they
would consider authentic,' he reasoned, 'And any illusions about consensus are
likely to be dispelled pretty quickly' (Kauffman, 1992, pp. 36–7).

US Press Reaction

There is no doubt that the protests about the film turned what would have
been just another Hollywood movie into a news story in its own right. No film
critic wrote a review of the film without mentioning the controversy. Whether
the hype also conditioned the critics to respond negatively to the film is a
moot point, but what is certain is that the majority of the reviews were
dismissive, and many were far more concerned with the film's misogyny than
its homophobia, which also chimed with some of the views expressed by
protesters. Tammy Bruce, president of the Los Angeles chapter of the
National Organization for Women, had described the film as 'so blatant in
its misogyny it is like a lynching' and that its message was that 'women are

dangerous and smart and can't be trusted' (cited in Horn, 1992, p. A5). 'Less homophobic than misogynist, more ridiculous than not' was J. Hoberman's verdict in the *Village Voice*. 'Every woman in the film is not only a possible or actual killer but a potential lesbian,' he noted. 'The running joke is that each, however, can be temporarily awed by the power of Douglas's wand' (Hoberman, 1992, p. 55). Janet Maslin (1992a) felt the film was 'far too bizarre and singular to be construed as homophobic'. For the *New Yorker,* Terrence Rafferty wondered, 'Will the movie take its smarmy misogyny all the way, or will it pull back in the end?', before concluding: 'It goes all the way' (Rafferty, 1992, p. 83). The *Los Angeles Times* reviewer agreed that the movie was 'more contemptuous of women in general than specifically anti-gay' (Turan, 1992). Other papers also deployed the accusation of misogyny, including the *New York Times* (Maslin, 1992a), the *Austin Chronicle* ('female sexuality, as usual, is the source of all evil') (Maher, 1992), the *Washington Post* ('a panting peep at the misperceptions and clichés surrounding female sexuality') (Kempley, 1992) and the *Spokane Chronicle* ('it's anti-lesbian and anti-female with a vengeance') (Lovell, 1992). Meanwhile, in the deeply conservative state of Alabama, the reviewer for the *TimesDaily,* noting her surprise at the lack of public response to the film, suggested that the film actually 'condescends to people in general, both men and women, straight or gay' and suggested the 'manner in which it portrays all single people as neurotic nymphomaniacs' was in itself 'offensive' (Hamby, 1992). Several critics, similarly unimpressed with the film's gender politics, noted that it presented a 'classic male fantasy' in the form of Catherine Tramell, described in the *Pittsburgh Post-Gazette* as 'a female temptress who is beautiful, overwhelmingly sexy and available, and happens to have $110 million in the bank' (Anderson, 1992, p. 3).

Others were perturbed by the film's nasty and gratuitous edge, and it was variously described as 'a harsh, angry, mean-spirited thriller [...] a cold-hearted, manipulative film' (Anderson, 1992, p. 3), 'arid and artless and base', glorifying brutality and perpetuating film violence (Dudek, 1992, p. 3D), and 'exhilarating, exhausting and seductively repellent' (Goodman, 1992, p. 17). In

Time magazine, Richard Schickel deplored the 'chilly, self-conscious sleekness' of the film's production design and the 'heartless and relentless thrill seeking of Paul Verhoeven's direction' (Schickel, 1992, p. 65).

When films receive a range of reviews, good and bad, the reception is often routinely described as 'mixed'. *Basic Instinct,* though certainly not unique, was at least unusual for the amount of individual reviews it received that could each be described as mixed: for a remarkable number of reviewers, the film seemed to provoke conflicting responses. Many recognised it as essentially trashy, but nevertheless oddly captivating. The *Austin Chronicle* described it as 'fascinating, if stupid and stylish, if shallow' (Maher, 1992). Desson Howe in the *Washington Post* found it 'predictable' and 'surprisingly uninvolving' (Howe, 1992), and *Entertainment Weekly* thought it 'mechanical and routine' (Gleiberman, 1992, p. 50). Glenn Lovell dismissed it as 'hilariously over-sexed' but at the same time admitted that, 'it's already near the top of this reviewer's I'll-detest-myself-in-the-morning pleasures' (Lovell, 1992).

Several critics, perhaps prompted into a backlash by the early hype about the record-breaking fee paid to Eszterhas, commented unfavourably on his screenplay. It was frequently dismissed as implausible: for Diane White, the film was 'so stupid it's difficult to take seriously' (White, 1992, p. 69). Owen Gleiberman even went so far as to suggest that Verhoeven 'must have decided to play the clunky, implausible script as a semi-joke' (1992, p. 50). Kenneth Turan felt that the film seemed 'less and less plausible the more convoluted it becomes' (1992). A few found the creakiness of the plot less of an obstacle to enjoyment of the film: 'as weirdly implausible as it is intensely visceral' was the judgment of one reviewer (*Variety,* 1992). However, a consensus also emerged among a number of critics that, while many of the film's weaknesses could be pinned on its screenplay, the director provided some redeeming features. Maslin (1992a) conceded that, '"Basic Instinct" transfers Mr. Verhoeven's flair for action-oriented material to the realm of Hitchcockian intrigue, and the results are viscerally effective even when they don't make sense.' Dan DiNicola (1992) believed that the 'weaknesses in the plot' were hidden by Verhoeven's 'slick' direction and 'technical wizardry'. Roger Ebert, however, pinpointed the script's key flaw. Discussing the last shot of the ice-pick beneath the bed (while ensuring he did not give away the plot detail), he complained:

> It's not really the last shot technique that I object to. What bothers me is that the whole plot has been constructed so that every relevant clue can be read two ways. That means the solution, when it is finally revealed, is not necessarily true. It is simply the writer's toss of the dice. (Ebert, 1992)

Very occasionally, a reviewer would be more forgiving: Peter Travers (*Rolling Stone*), perhaps predictably given his readership, luxuriated in the film's kitsch qualities ('gory, lurid, brutally funny and without a politically correct thought in its unapologetically empty head') and cheered Verhoeven on as he indulged 'his own basic instinct for disreputably alluring entertainment' (Travers, 1992).

A frequent criticism of the performances in the film was that they failed to humanise the protagonists: Desson Howe described them as 'blunt, formulaic creations' (Howe, 1992); 'These actors seem driven less by real emotions than Eveready bunny batteries', quipped the *Washington Post* reviewer (Kempley, 1992). However, many praised Stone's performance, even when they were unimpressed by any other aspect of the film: *Variety* (1992) called it 'career-making' and *Rolling Stone* declared that while the film 'establishes Stone as a bombshell for the Nineties, it also shows she can nail a laugh or shade an emotion with equal aplomb' (Travers, 1992). Some critics singled out the interrogation ('a scene no one will forget any time soon' according to the *Washington Post*) (Kempley, 1992), and Stone's performance in it, as particularly worthy of praise: Rafferty (1992) noted that she played it 'with splendid comic malice'. On the other hand, Desson Howe found it was only Douglas's star presence that put 'any oomph' into his character, and 'It's only Stone's nudity that put anything into hers' (Howe, 1992). Janet Maslin (1992a) also bucked the trend when she suggested that Douglas's 'strong and involving performance holds the film together [and] helps to humanize his bionically beautiful co-star'. However, more often than not, reviewers compared Douglas's performance unfavourably with Stone's: 'Douglas's Nick [...] spends so much time drenched in anger and frustration that one begins to fear that his ever-tightening neck muscles will explode under the strain,' Turan remarked in his review for the *Los Angeles Times* (1992).

Basic Instinct and the UK Press

Although *Basic Instinct* sailed through the BBFC's certification process with an 18 rating, one would never have known it had had such an easy passage by reading the popular press. Of course, UK distributor Guild worked with the publicity the film had received in the US over the protests and then the censorship so that it could market it as an 'event movie' (Austin, 2002, p. 46). The *Daily Mail* made an early bid to stir up interest in the film, name-checking the twenty-year-old Marlon Brando film *Last Tango in Paris* (1972) for its report 'New "Last Tango" Upsets Censors' (Usher, 1992a). *Last Tango* had caused a press furore in 1972 and the Board had made token cuts of ten seconds to the film's depiction of anal sex before granting it an X. The *Mail*'s report claimed that, 'British censors are locked in battle with the makers of Basic Instinct, the most controversial film of the year, over explicit sex scenes', and that the Board had asked 'for several cuts to the movie'; it went on to claim that 'the film's makers are prepared to fight to get an uncut version into British cinemas'. Usher quoted Stone's complaint that she had felt she had been 'tricked' by Verhoeven in the filming of 'one particularly graphic scene', and Douglas's take on the film's cultural significance: 'We had to make it because everything is so repressive now .... It's like you can't do anything, you have to abstain. This film breaks down those barriers' (Usher, 1992a). The *Sun* was more accurate in its reporting a few days later: featuring comments from British distributor Paul Brett, the focus seemed to be chiefly on the public's first ever sight on screen of Michael Douglas's 'manhood'. 'Our version is 47 seconds longer than theirs', Brett is quoted as saying. 'We get to see Michael

Douglas's willy and also see him in a very explicit sex scene with Sharon Stone. Some of the most violent scenes were trimmed in America, but all these remain in the British version' (*Sun*, 1992).

Thomas Austin provides a thorough overview of the ways in which the marketing of the film played on a number of interlocking elements: the star power and broad-based appeal of Douglas, the presentation of Stone as both a sex symbol for men and an example of the empowered female for women; the 'controversial' subject matter including lesbianism, bondage and sexual violence; and the censorship battle over securing the film a rating in the US (Austin, 2002, pp. 46–50). In terms of minority groups' responses to the film, there was no replication of the kind of press exposure and demonstrations that had attended the release on the other side of the Atlantic. A report in the *Independent* quoted Rob Kemp, a spokesperson for UK gay pressure group OutRage!, who said that they were against a boycott of the film. However, Kemp continued,

> everyone should be aware that this is the latest in a line of 'Queersploitation films' coming out of Hollywood. It is time for Hollywood to break out from showing only one type of queer […] it is time for an even-handed approach. (Earle, 1992, p. 18)

The feminist periodical *Spare Rib* printed a scathing attack on the film's gender politics: '*Basic Instinct* is a blatantly misogynistic and homophobic film; it is a vicious piece of hatred and scapegoating and should be exposed as such.' Identifying the same pressure points noted by many activists in the US, Coffey remarked upon the film's identification of lesbianism with deviance and violence, and the fact that a key premise of the film is that 'women are dangerous, seductive and potentially destructive'; 'But never fear', she adds; 'Such women always get punished' (Coffey, 1992, p. 20). While she is right to identify the clichés, one could argue with Coffey's conclusion in the case of *Basic Instinct*. After all, though both Beth and Roxy come to unfortunate ends, Catherine survives. Neither could it be argued that she is somehow 'contained' or 'neutralised' at the close of the film, a familiar *noir* convention: although it may appear that Nick is living his fantasy of 'fuck[ing] like minks and liv[ing]

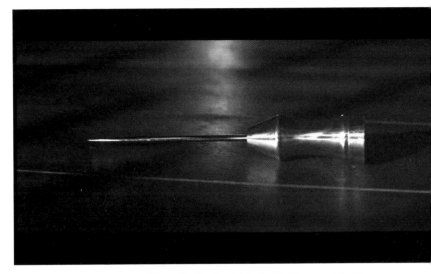

Figure 10: The ice-pick in the final frames of the film.

happily ever after', as he puts it, the final frames of the movie confirm that the ice-pick remains to hand (Figure 10).

The fact that *Basic Instinct* was released in a markedly more explicit version outside the US was reflected in the critical reaction. The tabloid *Daily Mirror*'s description of the film as 'probably the most sexually explicit and violent thriller you are ever likely to see in a public cinema' was typical (cited in Austin, 1999, p. 149); the reference to 'public cinema' carried the sly connotation of pornography, traditionally viewable only in private clubs and, more recently, on home video. The popular monthly film magazine *Empire* described the s ex scenes as 'going just about as far with a pair of mainstream Hollywood performers as it is currently permissible to go' (McIlheney, 1992, p. 20). The *Spectator* reviewer agreed that the film 'extends our idea of what can be accepted as mainstream' (Letts, 1992, p. 36). For Usher, it was 'an unholy or at least disgraceful alliance between suspense and porno movies' (1992b, p. 30) and Anthony Lane dismissed it as 'at the most […] teenage-horny' (1992, p. 18).

In general, although the film's sex scenes prompted a certain amount of reflective commentary, press reaction was broadly negative in the UK, probably even more so than it had been in the US. *City Limits* found it 'mind-numbingly clichéd', and 'a thoroughly undignified amoral depiction of the human race', singling out only Stone for praise ('well played considering the odds') (*City Limits*, 1992, p. 25). Philip French considered it passable as 'good night out' entertainment but, like many of the US critics, found fault with Eszterhas's script: 'the dialogue is often laughable and the plotting ludicrous' (1992, p. 52).

With regard to the film's gender politics, many of the UK critics echoed the verdict delivered on the other side of the Atlantic. Jeff Sawtell for the *Morning Star* condemned it as 'a deeply misogynist movie' (1992, p. 7), and the *Times* reviewer considered it 'a violent, misogynistic melodramatic stew …. See this film and a little more of your humanity gets chipped away,' Geoff Brown concluded (1992). Adam Mars-Jones declared the film 'too busy being misogynistic to have time for true homophobia' and made the sharply insightful observation that, 'Bisexuality in the film is essentially a symbol of woman's untrustworthiness' (Mars-Jones, 1992, p. 18). Both Geoff Brown and Hugo Davenport (*Daily Telegraph*) believed the film was exploitative, 'pandering to people's own basic instincts' (Brown, 1992); Davenport's review was headlined, 'A Basic Instinct for Big Profits' (Davenport, 1992). The *Daily Mail* critic concurred, using the rather ungainly headline, 'Following the Instinct to Make a Fast Buck, Basically' (Usher, 1992b, p. 30).

Although he felt the film's pace kept it a step ahead of its 'inherent implausibilities', Davenport still saw fit to sum it up as 'flash trash' … 'misanthropic rather than homophobic or misogynistic' (Davenport, 1992, p. 14). Alexander Walker agreed ('There isn't a speck of humanity in it') and singled out the date-rape scene for particularly vicious censure:

> filmed in a series of convulsive shocks, violent spasms, in which the woman's garments are ripped off her with such a sexy sound that you'd think her wardrobe came from the fashion house of Velcro. A normal woman would be filing charges. This one likes it. (Walker, A., 1992, p. 28)

Mars-Jones was another male critic offended by the scene, sardonically remarking that the character of Beth 'seemed more concerned with the rape as an index of his [Nick's] unhappiness than as a crime of which she was made the victim' (Mars-Jones, 1992, p. 18). Vanessa Letts was similarly cutting. 'It's not much fun […] watching Michael Douglas sodomising a lady psychiatrist against her will, especially when five minutes later she apologises for being aggressive' (Letts, 1992, p. 36).

A number of critics, however, in particular those representing the more popular press, took a stance on the film that overtly or implicitly rejected the approach taken by those preoccupied with the politics of gender and sexuality. The *Sun*, in typically mischievous mood, described it as 'One of those movies you hate yourself for liking. It's soft-porn. It's anti-gay. It's gratuitously violent. And they're the good points!' (Cox, 1992, p. 15). Effectively conceding that the film was, as the higher-minded critics suggested, exploitative, Cox quipped that, 'It's all done in the worst possible taste. And it's going to be huge!' (Cox, 1992, p. 15). Populist film enthusiast magazine *Empire* made a similar, deliberate attempt to distance itself from some of the more high-minded critiques of the movie: 'With the thought police closing in all the time,' it warned its readers, 'best enjoy this kind of mindless trash while you still have the chance' (McIlheney, 1992, p. 20). In one of the very few positive broadsheet reviews of the movie, Sheridan Morley ridiculed the protesters for taking it so seriously and pronounced it 'a perfectly gripping psycho-thriller with a couple of good twists' (1992, p. 62). Christopher Tookey took a similar approach in his review for the *Sunday Telegraph*, remarking that 'Some of the dialogue is hilariously crass' but concluding that, 'Basically, it's all good, dirty fun … *Basic Instinct* may not be a good film, but it's a thoroughly enjoyable bad one' (Tookey, 1992, p. III). When the hype was over and the dust settled, for better or worse, *Basic Instinct* achieved its primary purpose as a blockbuster, topping the UK box-office charts for 1992, and taking the number two spot in the annual home-video rental charts (Austin, 2002, p. 45).

Conclusion

Rebecca Feasey places *Basic Instinct* in a category she tags 'controversial blockbusters' alongside a number of other Hollywood films from the early 1990s such as *Indecent Proposal* (1993), *Disclosure* (1994) and *Striptease* (1995) (Feasey, 2003, p. 167). 'Each attempted to engineer public debate around sexual subject matter by offering fashionable, cutting-edge depictions of dangerous or "scandalous" erotic activity,' she argues (p. 168). Certainly *Basic Instinct* succeeded in provoking some very public debate, and in the spirit of no publicity is bad publicity, it capitalised on the storm it provoked among gay and lesbian and feminist pressure groups. It is difficult to make a definitive assessment of the impact *Basic Instinct* had on representations of homosexuality and bisexuality in Hollywood. What is not in doubt is the fact that the controversy that surrounded the film during pre-production, shooting and then on its release to cinemas raised awareness of the issue of homophobia, something that had been on the rise since the AIDS epidemic had seeped into the public consciousness.

One of the most enlightening commentaries came courtesy of Roger Ebert in his review of the film: noting how the recent film adaptation of *Fried Green Tomatoes* (1991) had been 'cravenly constructed' to 'obscure the story's obviously lesbian elements', he remarked on the irony that 'Hollywood is fearless in portraying lesbians as killer dykes, but gets cold feet with a story that might portray them (gasp!) as warm, good-natured and generous' (Ebert, 1992). Looking back on the film's impact with the benefit of hindsight, some critics are dismissive of the activists' campaigns against the movie. Jon Lewis believes that 'Street protests against *Colors* and *Basic Instinct* ... had the effect of making bad films important' (Lewis, 2000, p. 280). Even some activists objected to the strategies adopted by the likes of GLAAD: Anne-Marie Smith of Feminists against Censorship was sceptical of the effectiveness of the protests, pointing out that,

> Pro-censorship feminists made mistakes in the past, of assuming a
> direct link between images and actions, of excusing the viewer from

responsibility and portraying women always as victims of sexually explicit imagery. Images do not cause actions. (Alcorn, 1991, p. 17)

Ruth Picardie argued along similar lines in a piece for the *New Statesman:*

to claim that a film can 'inject' the gullible, mid-American viewer with homophobia is to interpret the relation between representation and action in precisely the same crude, causal way as a Jesse Helms or a Mary Whitehouse. For groups like Queer Nation who have defended the work of such gay artists as Robert Mapplethorpe, this is a disastrous argument in favour of censorship. (Picardie, 1992, p. 36)

Certainly there was at times a sense of censorship coming full circle in the objections to *Basic Instinct*'s representations of gender and sexuality, and a distinctly odd impression of an alliance – tacit, never acknowledged – of conservative Moral Majority types and the left, liberal feminists sharing common ground, albeit for very different reasons.

As I have shown, the critical reception for the film was predominantly sceptical. There was a widespread acknowledgment that the charges levelled against the film by feminist and gay activists were justified, even if some reviewers disagreed with the tactics adopted by the protesters. In the end, the controversy almost certainly succeeded in achieving nothing more than driving intrigued cinemagoers through the theatre doors in greater numbers. For the most part, the criticisms of the film (the weak and implausible plotting, the allegations of surface and no substance, wooden performances) fell on deaf ears, and the scandal and controversy that had gathered around the film from the very beginning served only to push *Basic Instinct* up the charts, establishing it as the most successful mainstream entry in the erotic thriller genre ever.

✖ Part 5

READING *BASIC INSTINCT*

Back to the Future

It's a scary time in the world. There are so many things that are
frightening – environmentally, psychologically, economically, sexually.
You can vent all your feelings through a movie like this. You can
vicariously let off steam. (Sharon Stone quoted in Johnson and Dwyer,
1992)

Watching *Basic Instinct* twenty years after it was made, perhaps what is
most striking is not necessarily what caused such a stir at the time – the
representations of bisexuality, the explicit sex scenes, the blending of
eroticism and graphic violence – but the way in which it functions as
a particularly lurid marker of its own era. The glossy sheen of the
cinematography, the shameless flaunting of great wealth and self-indulgence,
the odd combination of sexual licentiousness and anxiety (references to
condoms, the juxtaposition of enthusiastic sex and equally vigorous killing),
the pitting of men against women both in bed (Nick and Catherine) and in
the workplace (Nick and Beth), and across both contexts (Catherine in the
interrogation room, the Nick/Beth date rape): all of these seem very much of
their time, twenty years on. Nothing dates quite as fast as a movie trying to be
several steps ahead of its time. Older audience members today are most likely
to experience a sense of nostalgia as they watch it – ironic for a film that
seemed at the time both racily contemporary and retro, on account of its own
nostalgic gaze back at *noir* history. Younger audiences are likely to find it
rather alienating: the film more often than not strikes them as outmoded,
even camp (the night-club scene, with its plastic gaudiness, big hair,
80s-electro soundtrack and Nick's odd sartorial choices, being the most
obvious instance) (see Figure 11).

Figure 11: The night-club scene.

Even the stir the film caused in the gay and lesbian communities in some respects feels very much of its era. It remains on GLAAD's 'blacklist' as a film whose representation of bisexuality it classes as 'defamatory':

Basic Instinct: Tristar's 1992 motion picture blockbuster stands as one of the worst examples of biphobia ever put on a screen. Starring Sharon Stone and Michael Douglas, this thriller features two 'bisexual' women and a lesbian who lie, cheat, sleep, abuse drugs and murder their way through the entire movie. Reporting on the communities [sic] outrage, the San Francisco Examiner wrote that Stone's character was depicted as a 'permafrostic psychopath with the social grace of Norman Bates.' The movie demonized bisexuals, lesbians and women, painting them as predatory creatures. In a letter sent in March 1992, GLAAD told hundreds of movie critics nationwide that 'all the lesbian and bisexual characters in Basic Instinct are portrayed as potentially homicidal.' What

> made these depiction's [sic] worse was the lack of any positive gay, lesbian, bisexual or transgender people in Hollywood at all. GLAAD staged a number of highly visible protests at movie theaters around the country. (GLAAD archive, undated)

Twenty years on, sexuality seems much more plural, fragmented and hybridised than it did at the time *Basic Instinct* was made. And, of course, significant progress has been made towards the eradication of prejudice and homophobia, and towards the establishment of equality for people of all sexualities, even if there are many more battles still to be won. The sensitivity about Hollywood's representations of homosexuality and bisexuality is far less raw than it was when protesters picketed the 1992 Academy Award ceremony, even if openly gay actors and actresses remain a rarity among the ranks of the highest-profile stars.

In terms of film history, *Basic Instinct* stands as a fascinating example of neo-*noir* homage or pastiche of the classic *film noirs* of the 1940s and 1950s. However, the film remains of interest chiefly for the way it shifted popular perceptions of female violence in mainstream Hollywood film. It was made in a cultural climate that was responding to momentous changes in gender relations, changes reflected in a wave of female-led thrillers released at around the same time. This part of the book begins with an analysis of a couple of key 'psycho *femme*' films of the period in relation to *Basic Instinct* in order to offer a contextual reading of Verhoeven's film. The subsequent section explores the movie's representations of gender and power, chiefly via the relationship between Catherine and Nick. Catherine Tramell is more than a smart upgrade of the *femme fatale.* In some respects, she represents a turning point in representations of the violent woman. Yvonne Tasker describes Catherine as an icon of 'polymorphous perversity' (1994, p. 173), and compares Sharon Stone/Catherine Tramell to Linda Hamilton in *Terminator 2*, Sigourney Weaver in the *Alien* movies (1979–97) and Jamie Lee Curtis in *Blue Steel* (1989): 'These fantasy representations mobilize a range of readings, and the pleasures are many', she argues (p. 175). I will conclude with a consideration of the viewing pleasures that a film lambasted by many as homophobic can offer to a variety of audiences regardless of gender and sexuality.

Basic Instinct and the Violent Woman

The position of women in American society had been undergoing significant changes in the decade leading up to the release of *Basic Instinct*, and those shifts were continuing to make their impact felt in the early 1990s. At the beginning of the 1980s, the lurch to the political right signalled by the election of Ronald Reagan to the presidency was one of the most important factors in the failure of the Equal Rights Amendment (ERA) which had proposed legislation intended to guarantee the rights of all US citizens under the law regardless of gender. The ERA can be traced back to the 1920s, but it was not adopted by the Senate until 1972, with a seven-year deadline to complete ratification at state level, a process requiring three-quarters of state legislatures to adopt the Amendment. Supporters of the Amendment remained frustrated in their attempts to establish constitutional recognition of the need for equal rights for women. The states that failed to ratify were mostly midwestern and southern states, and the Republican opposition to ERA was rooted in social conservatism in general, and related to issues such as abortion, gay rights and family values, in particular. The ugly face of misogyny was most evident in the anti-abortion campaigns of the 1980s (as well as blockades, clinics were subjected to bombings and arson attacks, and employees were terrorised and assaulted).

In spite of political efforts across the board to roll back the advances made over the preceding fifteen or twenty years in women's rights, and in spite of the insistence by the Religious Right and associated factions that wives should submit to husbands and embrace the role of homemaker, clearly some changes were afoot. Sheila Rowbotham notes that 'Women's representation in the workforce increased from 51 to 57 per cent' in the 1980s, and by the end of the decade, '73.2 per cent of married women with children between six and seventeen were in paid employment' (Rowbotham, 1997, p. 524). When in *The Hand That Rocks the Cradle* (1992) Marlene (Julianne Moore) remarks to her friend Claire (Annabella Sciorra) that, 'These days a woman can feel like a failure if she doesn't bring in fifty grand a year and still make time for blow jobs and a homemade lasagne', she sums up the gender *Zeitgeist* better than any graph or table of statistics could. Indeed, with women making up nearly two-thirds of the minimum-wage workforce in 1989 (Rowbotham, 1997, p. 525), the situation was even worse than comfortable middle-class Marlene could imagine, and it was in this decade that the term 'glass ceiling' was coined to express the way in which women were almost always blocked from the higher rungs of career ladders.

For the character of Catherine Tramell in *Basic Instinct*, of course, none of this is an issue. The film remains locked in a solipsistic fantasy world, a northern California of clifftop beach-houses, his and hers Picassos and hers and hers Ferraris. Nevertheless, an understanding of women's evolving roles in society, in the family, and especially in relation to men is important if we are to find a way of reading between the lines (or looking between the frames) of such a box-office phenomenon as *Basic Instinct*. Catherine, Roxy, Beth and even the fleeting figure of Hazel Dobkins are fascinating for what they reveal about attitudes towards women in a film written, directed and produced by men, working within an industry that has itself, historically, been conditioned by heavily patriarchal structures and ideologies.

As a number of commentators and critics have noted, Catherine Tramell is only one in a series of dangerous women that appeared in Hollywood thrillers around the end of the 1980s and the beginning of the 1990s. The progenitor is probably *Fatal Attraction,* which pitted straying husband Dan (Michael Douglas again) against his casual-date-turned-obsessive-lover Alex (Glenn Close). Douglas would find himself in a similar predicament a few years after *Basic Instinct* when seduced by his boss Demi Moore in *Disclosure* . One commentator reflected at the time of its release that *Basic Instinct* 'has been cast as a metaphor for the 1990s. Where *Fatal*

Attraction, which also starred Douglas, spoke to the dangers of infidelity, *Basic Instinct*, it is argued, says that simply having sex is dangerous' (Tran, 1992, p. 6).

Fatal Attraction certainly offers a potentially intriguing analysis of the shifting balance of power between men and women at the time. New York attorney Dan seems to be ensconced in blissful domesticity with wife Beth (Anne Archer) and their six-year-old daughter, but has his head turned by the capable, confident publisher's editor Alex. Alex is powerful and confrontational in boardroom meetings, and her sassiness instantly attracts Dan, whose wife is seen in strongly contrasting settings (in the bathroom, making up in a mirror as they prepare for an evening out, attending to their daughter, or working in the kitchen). Taking advantage of his family's absence over a weekend, he embarks on what he imagines will be a no-strings, weekend affair with Alex. However, Alex clearly has very different ideas and when he tries to break it off, she first slashes her wrists and later informs Dan that not only is she pregnant with his child but she intends to keep the baby. As Dan continues with his stonewalling strategy, Alex spirals out of control and embarks on a campaign terrorising Dan, his family, infamously via some impromptu cookery involving the family pet. A sexually proactive and independent woman is rapidly transformed into a neurotic dependant who turns suicidal when her man tries to leave. Later, when Dan queries his parenthood of Alex's unborn child, she retorts that she is quite sure, 'because I don't sleep around', confronting the assumptions that Dan (and, perhaps, the audience) would have made earlier in the narrative. Dan flees the sexually liberated Alex and retreats to Beth and the cosy domesticity she represents, symbolised by their new home outside the city, complete with porch and white picket fence. As Dan's life continues to fall apart (he is forced to admit the affair to Beth) and Alex is transformed into something more akin to a slasher-movie villain than a recognisable human being, we are confronted with a scenario in which one sane man is placed at the centre of a maelstrom of raging female hormones. It reaches its climax as Alex breaks into the family home and attempts to murder Beth, with a violent confrontation ensuing between the two women claiming ownership over him. There was some agonising over how to shoot the film's ending – the final cut had Dan intervening just in time to save Beth, then drowning Alex in the bath. When Alex revives (in a classic slasher-villain move), Beth shoots her dead; the original ending (later included on the DVD release) had Alex committing suicide and framing Dan for her murder: however, this uncompromisingly downbeat ending, with the implication of Dan's subsequent arrest, did not please test audiences.

The film plays with a number of different cultural preoccupations and anxieties, including the status of women in the workplace and the implications of casual sex in a world where the AIDS epidemic was rewriting the rules of engagement. Derry notes that the issue of AIDS 'hangs over the film like a dim spectre'. He continues:

> In the era in which Nancy Reagan's 'Just Say No' dictum against drugs has become the watchword of a generation and *Zeitgeist* of the decade [...] *Fatal Attraction* becomes a clear, cautionary tale. Sexual intercourse can literally kill as surely as can Alex's knife-wielding psychopath. Dan's original sin, certainly, is that he *didn't* just say no. Thus, *Fatal Attraction* seems to suggest that we must retreat from the Sexual Revolution and the New Morality and return to a happier and simpler time in which the nuclear family prospered. (Derry, 1988, p. 100)

In the end, the film settles rather complacently for the status quo, although Glenn Close was recently quoted suggesting that her performance in the movie was responsible for keeping potential philanderers in line: 'Men still come up to me and say, "You scared the s*** outta me"' (Moodie, 2007). She mused that the character of Alex, lambasted by feminists on its release, is now more likely to be considered a 'heroine'. At the time, however, as Susan Faludi notes, screenings of the film were often accompanied by shouts from the audience cheering Dan on in the final showdown: '"Do it, Michael. Kill her already. Kill the bitch"' (Faludi, 1993, p. 140). For Faludi, and other feminists at the turn of the decade, *Fatal Attraction* represented part of the cultural backlash against women's progress towards equal rights. Faludi argued that conservative social and political forces, and in turn the media and popular culture, made every effort to reverse that progress. Such efforts included an initiative to portray women's new-found freedom and autonomy as the cause of a supposed disillusionment and discontent among contemporary women, epitomised in a character like Alex.

Faludi described the common themes in Hollywood's portrayal of women in the 1980s thus:

> women were set against women; women's anger at their social circumstances was depoliticised and displayed as personal depression instead; and women's lives were framed as morality tales in which the 'good mother' wins and the independent woman gets punished. (Faludi, 1993, p. 141)

To that list, as we moved into the 1990s, Faludi could have added the figure of the lethal woman. Alex may have been seen at the time as a single, working woman who was supposed to be 'the source of all evil' as Close puts it, but the image of the deadly female took on a number of different incarnations. The year that *Basic Instinct* was released, entries in the genre included the Lolita-esque Drew Barrymore character in *Poison Ivy* (1992) seducing her friend's father, Jennifer Jason Leigh's lonely psychotic double (Hedy) to Bridget Fonda's young career woman (Ally) in *Single White Female* (1992) and the vengeful nanny (Rebecca De Mornay) taking over the gentle middle-class mother's life (Annabella Sciorra) in *The Hand That Rocks the Cradle*.

In the latter, De Mornay's husband, gynaecologist Victor Mott (John de Lancie), molests Claire Bartell (Sciorra) at her pre-natal exam and when he is reported and accused by several more women, takes his own life. His wife, heavily pregnant, collapses when she hears of his death, and loses both her baby and her ability to bear children in the aftermath. Reinventing herself as Peyton Flanders, she works her way into Claire's confidence as a nanny to

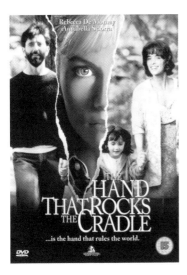

newborn Joe and young daughter
Emma (Madeline Zima). Peyton
proceeds to take over Claire's family,
forming a bond with Emma, illicitly
breastfeeding the baby and
attempting (unsuccessfully) to seduce
Claire's husband Michael (Matt
McCoy). Like Catherine Tramell,
Peyton manipulates and scripts the
behaviour of the characters around
her in order to engineer the situation
to fit her vengeful plans. When her
identity is eventually discovered and
Claire confronts her, Peyton takes on
the contours of the classic slasher-
movie villain (reminiscent of Alex in

Figure 12: The lethal-woman movie
of the early 1990s.

Fatal Attraction, and complete with *Psycho*-style screeches of strings to punctuate her actions). Through the entire climax of the film, her violence is shocking in a way analogous to the blonde killer's violence in the opening scene of *Basic Instinct*; however, her weapons are not sharp but blunt and used as bludgeons (a shovel, a poker), objects that require (and get) brute force. In the final analysis, the extent of Peyton's psychosis is never quite clear. When she whispers in Claire's ear, in the midst of the climactic fight, 'When your husband makes love to you, it's my face he sees; when your baby is hungry, it's my breast that feeds him', it could be that it is merely a taunt; on the other hand, it could be on a par with Hedy's Doppelgänger-ing of Ally's life in *Single White Female*. In both Peyton and Hedy's case, it is enough that their profoundly strange behaviour is just that – alien, unfathomable – and as impenetrable, finally, as Catherine's psychotic violence (or Roxy's, or Hazel's) in *Basic Instinct*.

Basic Instinct as Postmodern Neo-*Noir*

The psycho *femme* genre is a significant development of the thriller genre around the turn of the decade, and one in which *Basic Instinct* sits comfortably, although Verhoeven's film has much deeper roots. Specifically, it belongs in the tradition of *film noir*, and the character of Catherine Tramell is frequently invoked as a revamped *femme fatale*. Joe Eszterhas's autobiography reveals that the film began specifically as an exercise in genre-writing. Between the writer's decision to work quite consciously (albeit playfully) within generic conventions and Verhoeven's indebtedness to certain key movies inside, or on the perimeter, of the *noir* tradition (in particular, a number of Hitchcock films), one might be led to expect a rather contrived movie. Indeed, Linda Ruth Williams suggests that 'the exemplary film of its genre is also a parodic interrogation of that genre' (Williams, 2005, p. 164). A full understanding of the way *Basic Instinct* operates relies upon at least a working knowledge of the *noir* tradition. The ways in which Eszterhas, Verhoeven and (to an extent) the film's actors pay homage to, and at the same time subvert, *noir* conventions, particularly in relation to Catherine, are vital to an understanding of the games the film plays with gender and sexuality.

Bould, Glitre and Tuck point out that the *noir* genre has always been hard to pin down definitively, 'with critics never quite agreeing upon whether it is a genre or a style or a theme or a mood or a form or a texture or a cycle .... And yet somehow, film noir seems instantly recognisable' (2009, p. 3). Bearing in mind the caveat about the slipperiness of the term, it is possible to list the key conventions of *film noir,* while agreeing that not all films falling under the definition will necessarily include every one of them. In terms of character, the classic *film noir* usually features a 'tough detective in an urban milieu' as protagonist (Walker, M., 1992, p. 9), often morally ambivalent, or compromised by his surroundings. It is a typology that suits Michael Douglas's portrayal of Nick Curran, shaded by a history of alcoholism, accidental shootings and disciplinary action, perfectly. Andrew Spicer's summary locates a number of other male archetypes, including the male victim (usually the dupe of the *femme fatale*) and the damaged male (often maladjusted veterans or rogue cops), and the character of Gus slots quite comfortably somewhere in between the two (Spicer, 2002, p. 89). The dangerous woman, or *femme fatale,* using her sexuality to ensnare the hero – 'overpoweringly desirable, duplicitous and sexually insatiable' (Spicer, 2002, p. 90) – is a vital figure, and of course is central to *Basic Instinct,* but *noir* films also often include a domesticated woman set in opposition to the sexually transgressive *femme fatale* (Walker, M., 1992, pp. 13–14), a role filled by the character of Nick's therapist and former lover Beth. In narrative terms, critics often note that containment of the *femme fatale* is a key feature of these films. Typically, the dangerous woman at the centre of the plot is either killed, married off, or otherwise safely neutralised by the end of the movie, and this is perhaps one of the major departures from generic patterns represented by Verhoeven's film (although one alternative ending was much less subversive of the tradition; see p. 20).

Considering the phases of the *noir* genre, it is possible to identify *Basic Instinct*'s progenitors more specifically. In many foundational studies of *film noir*, the 'classic' period is generally understood as having been bookended by John Huston's *The Maltese Falcon* (1941) and Orson Welles's *Touch of Evil* (1958). However, it is the later wave, sometimes identified as neo-*noir*, which is a more familiar reference point for *Basic Instinct*. It begins with Lawrence Kasdan's *Body Heat* and *The Postman Always Rings Twice* (both 1981), hesitates, and then takes flight at the end of the decade via the likes of *Kill Me Again* (1989), *After Dark, My Sweet*, *The Grifters* and *The Hot Spot* (all 1990), *Deceived* and *A Kiss before Dying* (both 1991), and, in the same year as Verhoeven's film, *Red Rock West* (1992), *Body of Evidence* and many more. According to Todd Erickson, the neo-*noir* 'incorporates and projects the narrative and stylistic conventions of its progenitor onto a contemporary canvas' (1996, p. 321). Both *Body Heat* and *The Postman Always Rings Twice* could be classified, broadly, as 'revivalist' (Spicer, 2002, p. 150), although the former is far more playful and imaginative in its deployment of traditional *noir* conventions than the latter.

Moving from conventions to the more nebulous notion of theme, Charles Derry suggests the *noir* tone is defined by 'a cynical, existential *Weltanschauung*' (1988, p. 7), while Spicer sums up the genre's preoccupations as 'claustrophobia, paranoia, despair and nihilism' (2002, p. 64). Frequently, the protagonist is placed in the centre of a confusing web of intrigue, trying to make sense of events that are spiralling out of his control, and this is readily mappable onto Nick's predicament in *Basic Instinct*. Michael Walker also discusses a range of other elements, including interlocking sexual triangles (often between *femme fatale,* male dupe and domestic female) and a thematic focus on 'the darker areas of the psyche (obsession and neurosis are common preoccupations) … male sexual anxieties and … the pathology of male violence' (Walker, M., 1992, p. 38).

It is this latter preoccupation, inverted and skewed in fascinating ways, which is at the heart of *Basic Instinct*. Like so many movies of its genre – whether we consider that to be some variant of *noir*, thriller, or cop procedural – the milieux for the characters and the narrative of *Basic Instinct* is largely inhabited, dominated and driven by men. The gender dynamic, complicated by the film's focus on sexuality, means that, as Angela Galvin suggests, *Basic Instinct*'s narrative 'is less concerned with investigating the crime [Boz's death] than it is with investigating the emasculation of nineties man as revealed through the psyche of Nick, his psychotherapist (Beth Garner) and Catherine' (Galvin, 1994, p. 222). The ways in which the film plays with gender and power, and subverts some of the stereotypes of the *noir,* or neo-*noir* genre along the way, is the subject of the next part of the discussion.

Catherine and the *Femme Fatale* Archetype: The Threat to Patriarchy

A consideration of the movie's second scene – following on immediately from the opening, mysteriously context-free sex and death sequence – reveals how central masculinity is to the film. The dialogue is littered with macho joshing. Nick and Gus joke about the manner of Johnny Boz's death (noting the semen stains, Gus remarks, 'He got off before he got offed') and when Nick takes a closer look through the forensic officer's eyewear, he nods, 'Very impressive'. Similar banter dominates all the scenes involving the police officers: following the autopsy report, Boz is summed up as someone who 'liked his girls, liked his drugs [and] liked his rock'n'roll', and in the same scene, Nick, who was spotted leaving the bar the night before in the company of Beth, is the butt of a number of jokes about his relationship with her: 'You look like dogshit,' Walker (Denis Arndt) tells him; 'No,' responds Gus, 'He looks a little shrunk is all.' 'And not just in the head,' adds Harrigan (Benjamin Mouton), another officer. When Walker informs his men that he wants 'psychological input' on the case, Gus remarks to Nick that 'You're already getting psychological input, Hoss.' Typical male bravado about sexual conquests, then, is very much present and politically incorrect, and even here the dialogue carries a subtext that takes potshots at Nick's virility. There is the obvious phallic implication of 'shrunk' (implying Beth emasculating him), as well as the male/female inversion of Nick as the one being penetrated ('psychological input'); all this ironically set against the preceding sequence depicting Nick's sexual assault on Beth in the date-rape scene.

By-numbers tensions between the protagonist and his superior officers are also in evidence: though on good terms, if short-leashed, with Lieutenant Walker (Walker insists that Nick keeps his appointment with the department psychologist), there is bristling mutual hostility between Nick and Captain Talcott (Chelcie Ross). *Basic Instinct* also plays out a familiar opposition of hard-working, blue-collar police officers picking up the pieces left in the wake of the lifestyle choices of the rich and debauched; the early 1990s vintage further accentuates the sense of affluence and indulgence and gives it a substance-abuse slant, too – when Talcott insists that Boz was a 'civic-minded, very respectable rock'n'roll star' with connections to the Mayor, Nick makes a quip about the 'civic-minded, very respectable cocaine' found at the bedside. Nick and Gus, on the other hand, form a typical detective partnership: the younger, leaner, edgier, more cynical Nick is complemented by the older, thickset, easy-going Gus, whose world-weariness tastes less bitter. The sense of male camaraderie is further enhanced by their terms of address: Nick calls him 'cowboy', and his partner refers to him as 'hoss' (the homoerotic subtext, explored by Celestino Deleyto (1997) and others, is discussed further below; see pp. 126–8).

The film's effort to establish a distinctively male sense of ease and confidence in the crime-scene sequence has an immediate pay-off when Gus and Nick travel to their first port of call on the trail of Catherine Tramell. From the very beginning of their investigation, they are wrong-footed, their masculine overconfidence rapidly undermined by the way their female suspects respond to their questioning and, perhaps just as importantly, by the fact that the women are clearly underwhelmed by their profession and their male swagger. Both Nick and Gus are fooled into assuming that the woman who first greets them at the house on Divisadero is Catherine Tramell. Roxy, perched above them on the staircase, toys with them, happy to play up to their assumption that she is Catherine (an uninformed audience might assume the same). When she finally deigns to directs them to Catherine's beach-house at Stinson, her parting shot as they leave ('You're wasting your time. Catherine didn't kill him') finds her still standing in the centre of the staircase, her aggressive stance compared by Camille Paglia to that of a gunslinger:[31] an appropriate metaphor for Cowboy and Hoss as they saddle up for the next leg of their journey.

On their first drive out to Stinson, the car is seen weaving its way up through the hills in extreme long shot, and the score's main theme, familiar from the opening scene, returns. The impression is of Catherine drawing the men into her web. When they receive no answer at the door, it is Nick who spies a path around the side of the property, and for a moment, it would seem that they are establishing the upper hand, taking Catherine by surprise, as they walk down towards decking overlooking the sea, where she sits, her back to them. However, she seems unsurprised by their arrival. When Nick calls her name ('Ms. Tramell'), she turns with a half-mocking, faintly amused face (see Figure 13), then simply turns back to look out to sea; she does not reply and does not invite them to join her; and when Nick attempts an introduction, she

Figure 13: Nick and Gus's first encounter with Catherine.

cuts him off ('I know who you are') and, like Roxy, wrong-foots him by leap-frogging several places ahead: 'So, how did he die?', she asks, her tone and manner remaining puzzlingly neutral. As the conversation continues, it is obvious that the detectives' suspicions are being roused, something that seems to cause Catherine no anxiety whatsoever. Instead she mocks them, and when they tell her how he died, she seems to find it mildly amusing. As the questioning continues, Catherine deploys another weapon that will prove particularly effective in the later interrogation scene. Asked how long she had been dating Boz, she replies, matter of factly, 'I wasn't dating him; I was fucking him.' Asked if there was anyone with her the previous evening (so the detectives can establish whether she has an alibi), she replies, 'No. I wasn't in the mood last night.' The original script reads, 'No. I wasn't in the mood to have sex with anyone last night,' which is clumsy and overly literal; in Stone's well-judged delivery, the implication is clear enough, so clear in fact that it already sounds as if she is coming on to Nick, Gus or both of them. Her frankness – her tactic of apparently hiding nothing, which will continue to serve her well – conditions her response when Nick asks whether she is sorry he's dead. 'Yeah,' she replies. 'I liked fucking him.' The scene ends and Nick and Gus drive away from Stinson exchanging glances and rather bewildered smiles, evidently at something of a loss. 'Nice girl,' Gus offers at last, and they smirk, reassuring one another that the threat of female power has been boxed away with a safe, patronising label. At least, for now.

As the film proceeds and Catherine reels Nick in, the extent to which he has fallen under her thrall is given an index via the comments of other representatives of the masculine culture to which Nick belongs. When he tries to convince his superior officer that it was Catherine who killed Nilsen in an attempt to frame him, Walker is exasperated, and tells Nick to get away, get some sun and 'get her out of your system [...]. She is screwing with your head, Nick,' he tells him. 'Stay away from her.' As matters proceed, Gus becomes increasingly infuriated with Nick's helplessness: 'Well, she got that *magnum cum laude* pussy that done fried up your brain,' he remarks, conflating her diabolical intelligence and her irresistible sex appeal. Of course, part of what makes Catherine so extraordinary is the fact that she proves irresistible to just about anyone who crosses her path, male or female. Nowhere is this better illustrated than in the infamous interrogation scene, which I will consider in detail in a moment.

In a number of interviews, Verhoeven has suggested that the best way to understand Catherine is as 'the devil', since it is the only way to explain her apparent omniscience, even omnipotence, notably in her setting up of the film's climax. Here, she manages to set up a rendezvous between Gus and Beth, kill Gus, leave evidence to incriminate Beth and, presumably, ensure that Nick shoots Beth, while returning to Beth's apartment to plant further evidence (and erase taped messages from her phone's answering machine) before arriving back at Nick's apartment in time for his return. There are scattered references in the script, notably by Dr Lamott (who 'teaches the pathology of psychopathic behaviour at Stanford') in his hilariously straight-faced assessment of the suspect's psychological profile. 'A devious, diabolical mind' is the phrase he uses. Even more unintentionally funny is the line poor Jeanne Tripplehorn has to deliver as she shouts her desperate warning about Catherine after the departing Nick: 'She's evil! She's brilliant!' Williams sees the 'devil' rhetoric as at the heart of the conflicted responses that Catherine can provoke among feminists in particular: 'On this hinges *Basic Instinct*'s contradiction for feminism', she claims.

> [A]s female // demon Catherine is prime exhibit in Verhoeven's *Malleus Maleficarum*, and evidence for feminism's case against him; but as demon in a universe which primarily values the demonic, she rules supreme, thus also functioning as celebratory role-model. (Williams, 2005, pp. 165–6)

The Interrogation Scene

The interrogation scene may remain most famous, and most controversial, for the inclusion of the revealing shot of Catherine Tramell/Sharon Stone. The genesis of that shot has been widely disputed and discussed (see pp. 15–17). However, it is most *interesting* for the way in which it represents the triumph of the *femme fatale* not just over the male protagonist, but over a room full of men. From the moment she enters the room, Catherine is the focus. Her white, blonde and gold colours are set starkly against the blue, black and grey of the interior of the room and of the men, decked out in a similar palette. Furthermore, the scene is very overtly staged:[32] there is nothing naturalistic about the way the room is presented, or the way the set is dressed. The lighting is particularly melodramatic: footlights illuminate the rear wall, the steely blues and greys work with the light coming through the criss-cross ceiling panels above to enhance the sense of the room as a prison. The way Catherine is lit, and the men comparatively shadowed, conveys a sense of theatre, with Catherine cast as performer and the cops as the audience (Figure 14).

Figure 14: The interrogation scene.

From the beginning, Catherine takes control. Told by Officer Corelli (Wayne Knight) that she cannot light up a cigarette in the room, Catherine raises a quizzical eyebrow and retorts, 'What are you gonna do? Charge me with smoking?' Her challenge is followed by a reaction shot from Nick and Gus, who look across to Corelli. He has nothing to say in reply, and his eyes fall. Asked about the nature of her relationship with Johnny Boz, she replies that she had sex with him for about a year and a half; there is a slight pause before she adds, 'I liked having sex with him,' as the camera closes in on her. 'He wasn't afraid of experimenting,' she continues. Whereas the police questioning is structured to leave gaps to allow leading questions to drag out replies that might give away more than the suspect would like, Catherine appropriates the gaps for her own ends. Already there is a sense among the men that this might be 'more than we needed to know', but her replies are designed to establish her willingness to assert her sexuality, and to knock her inquisitors off-balance. In particular, the fact that she is not ashamed to prioritise sexual pleasure is deeply unnerving for her male interrogators. When Corelli enquires, 'You ever … errr … engage in any sadomasochistic activity?' he not only averts his eyes but even removes his glasses (a gesture of vulnerability and, a Freudian would probably add, an admission of his emasculation, blindness being identified with castration). Catherine, well aware of the extent of the control she has already established, particularly over Corelli, leans forward to reply, as if favouring him with an intimacy she denies the other men: 'Exactly what did you have in mind, Mr. Corelli?' The seductive subtext is so overt that it hardly qualifies as such. At the end of her next elaboration ('Johnny liked to use his hands … I like hands and fingers'), the film cuts to a long shot of Corelli, Walker and Talcott; Walker has stood up to fetch a cup of water from the water cooler situated behind them, and Corelli is mopping his brow with a handkerchief. The effect is so exaggerated it verges on the comical, and is one of the reasons why the scene has been so frequently parodied: Catherine's brazen talk seems to have quite literally raised the temperature in the room by several degrees, and the men can no longer keep themselves under control.

When Nick takes the lead with questioning, the camera cuts between close-ups of him and Catherine, their faces framed centrally, giving the sense of the two of them in direct engagement – as if the others in the room are not even there. When she slaps Nick down again ('I thought you said you liked men to use their hands' – 'No, I said I liked *Johnny* to use his hands'), she follows up with a tonal shift that goes from sharp retort to casual intimacy: 'I don't make any rules, Nick; I go with the flow.' Once again, Catherine manages to make a simple reply sound like a sexual invitation. She is equally forthright and unashamed as she admits to having used cocaine with Boz, even turning the question back against the men, in her most audacious move yet: 'Have you ever fucked on cocaine, Nick?', she asks. 'It's nice.' Nick looks up, and then there is a cut to Corelli and Talcott who are offering Nick accusatory stares, while the soundtrack enhances the suspense. It is at this point that the camera reverts to Catherine, in long shot, framed slightly to the right of centre, as she uncrosses her legs, never shifting her gaze from the men (Figure 15) – or rather from Nick in particular. She pauses with both feet on the floor and her legs slightly parted, and the camera cuts to Corelli (foreground) and the captain (background) as they realise what Catherine is allowing them to see: a view between her legs, knickerless, her vulva exposed. Corelli raises his head, his eyes fixed, and we cut back to his point of view except in a medium close-up of Catherine, from the chest down, with her naked vagina the focus (Figure 16); the glimpse is fleeting, and as she recrosses her legs we cut back to Corelli, his face still registering shock, arousal and disappointment at the fleeting nature of the flash (Figure 17); then back to Catherine in long shot, face still open yet giving nothing away. She swings her crossed leg provocatively as she completes her line ('It's nice'). Questioned again about her sexual morality – 'you didn't love him [Boz], even though you were fucking him' – her response is once again centred on her right to sexual autonomy: 'You still get the pleasure. Didn't you ever fuck anyone else when you were married, Nick?' she retorts, almost as a direct reference to the double standard about men and women's enjoyment of sex, or the traditional assumption of male entitlement to guilt-free infidelity.

Figure 15: Exposed, and the least vulnerable person in the room.

Figure 16: What Corelli sees ... .

Figure 17: ... And his reaction shot.

Interviewed ten years or more after the film was released, Verhoeven was quite clear about the gender politics of the interrogation sequence, as he understood them: 'That shot was the ultimate metaphor for the whole scene,' he told Linda Ruth Williams. 'Like, *this* is how I play you all, you drooling males! She basically plays these men and reduc[es] them to dwarves' (Williams, 2005, p. 246). On the other hand, not everyone would endorse this positive spin on the scene: Galvin notes that 'the women with whom I first watched the film saw the scene as a presentation of female vulnerability and powerlessness' rather than as a subversion of traditional sexual power relations (1994, p. 226). Galvin also criticises the representation of intimacy between women in the film, and notices that the Catherine–Roxy relationship is depicted almost exclusively as points on the triangle that also includes Nick, either arousing his or Roxy's jealousy (fondling her breast as he leaves her house, dancing provocatively with her at the night-club, and Roxy watching them have sex) (Galvin, 1994, p. 228).

Roxy's largely untold story is one of the film's most curious lacunae. Her death is briefly mourned by Catherine (or is it? It is difficult to distinguish between Catherine's real feelings and her performances). For the most part she functions as a plot device and as an index of Catherine's sexuality. Nick's confrontations with Roxy can also be seen as additional rounds in the gender and power game. After having sex with Catherine for the first time, Nick gets up from the bed and walks naked to the bathroom, where he washes his face. As he stands up, Roxy is revealed behind him in a confrontational stance (Figure 18): 'If you don't leave her alone, I'll kill you,' she tells him. Nick turns and faces her. He makes no attempt to cover himself up: in fact, his full frontal nudity, for Roxy's benefit, is very purposeful. The subtext ('but you don't have one of *these,* do you?') is loud and clear, and emphasised by his next line: 'Let me ask you something, Rocky [sic]. Man to man …'. Nick's words are probably as much in retaliation to the earlier meeting when Catherine embraced, kissed and fondled Roxy in front of him as much as they are an

Figure 18: Confrontation between Nick and Roxy.

instance of homophobia. The mispronunciation of her name as Rocky – which, regardless of the Sylvester Stallone connotation, is comically macho – is particularly blatant. He makes a further claim of ownership over Catherine when he follows up with the comment, 'I think she's the fuck of the century; what do you think?' The exchange that follows is another stage in the same proprietorial battle over Catherine, and a further implication on Nick's part that Roxy is no match for him as her sexual partner: 'You like watching, don't you?' he sneers; 'She likes me to watch,' Roxy replies. She stalks away and Nick strides manfully back to the bed, swaggering as much as any butt-naked man can without looking ridiculous.

Beth: The Domesticated Female

If Catherine represents the subversive potential of the liberated, empowered, polysexual woman, then Beth corresponds more closely to the *noir* archetype of the domesticated female, even if on the surface she seems to have a degree of authority and control. It is presumably no coincidence that the first encounter with Catherine is set in juxtaposition to Nick's first scene with Beth. In some senses, the roles are reversed: Beth becomes Nick, forced to take the initiative with the interrogation as she carries out a routine evaluation of his mental health. Nick is relatively cool and dismissive. When Beth asks about his personal life, he assumes this to be code for sex life (an analogue to the earlier dating/fucking quibble), and makes a reference to masturbation, coarsening the tone of the conversation considerably – although Catherine was consistently unapologetic, and Nick, by contrast, quickly apologises for the remark. Beth enjoys a degree of authority over Nick, since she is his psychologist assessing his fitness for work, and so effectively exerting control over much of what defines him as a man. However, his pleading with her to 'Let me out of here. Please,' and her hesitation and final assent do not give the impression that she holds the balance of power. Although she delivers the line almost as if she is granting a child a favour, the note of insincerity in his 'thank you', and what follows, further undermines Beth: as Nick stands up, swiftly turns on his heel, and heads for the door, she calls after him, 'I still miss you, Nick.' Nick hesitates with his hand on the door handle. Then, without a word, without even a glance back at her, he leaves, closing the door after him.

The triumph of the male over the seemingly authoritative, actually meekly dependent female continues as Nick meets up with Gus, and his partner asks him how it went. 'She misses me,' Nick scoffs. In the original screenplay, Gus's reply is a fairly neutral 'Hallelujah.' In the film, his reply is far more cutting and misogynistic: 'Boy, when that girl mates, it's for life.' The line is ironic, of course, given the way the narrative will play out. But it can also be interpreted as another attempt to establish male superiority, particularly in the wake of the first blood Catherine has drawn in her initial meeting with the two detectives.

Later, the argument between Nick and Beth that immediately precedes the discovery of Nilsen's body is conventional in terms of gendered responses: Nick is in control, initiating the end of the affair, insisting on her handing over the keys to his apartment. His assessment of their failed relationship, and his conclusion that going to bed ten or fifteen times together means that it wasn't 'memorable enough to carry an obligation', leads to her sudden, violent outburst. Her attack on Nick is presumably intended to mirror their earlier sex scene (see pp. 59–60): she forces him, arms up, against the wall, and as they struggle, he turns her around so her back is to him before he throws her across the room. Despite the fact that Nick has used brutal force in controlling her aggression, it is the passive Beth who apparently feels obliged to apologise. Nick, meanwhile, softens only a little as he dismisses her with a weary, 'Just go away, Beth.' When he is questioned the next day under suspicion of having murdered Nilsen, Beth has already forgiven him everything, it seems, and she provides him with an alibi. No doubt her willingness to jump to his defence is in part attributable to her sense of guilt over having given Nilsen his file; however, her decision to help Nick out of his perilous predicament is in keeping with her passive, domesticated victim role in the relationship.

Carol Siegel describes Beth as 'a whining embodiment of stereotypical femininity, always defined by powerless maternal fluttering or helpless dependence' (Siegel, 1995, p. 331). Beth fleetingly becomes a more enigmatic, potentially more imposing figure when details of her past emerge (including the death of her husband), and the movie puts her in the frame as a possible suspect. However, through a combination of creaky plot and indifferent acting, the charade remains unconvincing, and Beth lingers in the memory as the passive brunette flipside to Catherine's all-conquering blonde devil.

Basic Instinct's Viewing Pleasures

Thrillers such as *Fatal Attraction* and *Basic Instinct* that feature powerful female protagonists tend to provoke conflicted responses, particularly when those figures have strong associations with violence. Leighton Grist is in no doubt that *Fatal Attraction* sets up an 'opposition of good woman and *femme fatale* [which] works to naturalise a misogynistic denial of "transgressive" female (sexual) independence before a championing of woman's "traditional" subordinate domesticity' (1992, p. 276). On the other hand, Charles Derry is more ambivalent in his assessment. 'Is *Fatal Attraction* a feminist film?' he asks. 'Perhaps so: … [Alex is] the strongest and most interesting character in the film […] an intelligent, self-possessed career woman.' However, in the following paragraph, he muses, 'Is *Fatal Attraction* an antifeminist film? Perhaps so: …' and suggests that Alex's descent into psychosis marks her out as a 'monster', validating by contrast the 'ideological position of the bourgeois wife' Beth (Derry, 1988, p. 100), thus confirming the 'containment' argument Grist advocates.

One of the implications of postmodern approaches to film inter-pretation is the abandoning of any ambition to fix meaning, or to sift the 'true' meaning from the false ones. Attempts at pinning meaning down are rejected in favour of an open embrace of a multiplicity of meanings which are often competing or even mutually contradictory. This is certainly the implication of 'queer' readings of popular cinema, where versions that others might view as wilfully perverse are posited, and often surprising and radical reinterpretations of characters and situations are championed. If 'queer', as Julia Erhart suggests, 'was intended as a productively disruptive alternative to what was seen as the assimilationist and conservative aims of post-liberation movement majority gay culture' (Erhart, 2004, p. 173), then it is possible to read some of the strategies adopted in queer readings as viable alternatives to the approach that defined the initial controversy around *Basic Instinct*. That is to say, it may be possible to conceive of another way to confront, resist or counter 'offensive' representations in ways that do not take us down the route of either artistic censorship (the pressure groups' attempts to persuade the film-makers to make script changes) or boycotts (the demonstrations outside movie theatres). Clare Whatling sees the kind of alternative, 'against the grain' readings offered by queer critics as

> an attempt to turn the dominant back on itself, to steal the terms that have formerly oppressed us, utilising the abject in the best of Kristevan (1982) senses as a productive and ambiguous category for the cultivation of a productive and ambiguous lesbian desire. (Whatling, 1997, pp. 80–1)

Beth may be difficult to recuperate in any meaningful way as anything other than a tired Hollywood cliché, but Catherine is a different case entirely. Clare Whatling's assessment of her, for example, acknowledges her as a 'man-eating monster' but adds:

> to many of the lesbian spectators who watched her wreak havoc in the world of Nick Curran, [she is also] wealthy, independent and damned sexy. Heterosexual male fantasy nightmare she may be, but her character is also fraught with lesbian erotic possibilities should the lesbian-identified (or otherwise-) identified spectator choose to plumb them. (Whatling, 1997, p. 79)

Whatling singles out a remark by one lesbian spectator, Cherry Smyth, concerning the interrogation scene's famous flash: 'I found that scene really hot. She's saying, "I'm going to get you with my pussy." That's great. It made me laugh – Sharon Stone was so sexy and powerful.' Smyth proceeds to reflect on the reaction of a male spectator sitting next to her, who did not seem to find the scene funny; she muses that he might have been 'a politically correct male trying to figure out what exactly his reaction should be' (McClellan, 1992, p. 91, cited in Whatling, 1997, p. 102). Galvin also quotes Smyth to make the same point and notes that the film has tended to be critiqued more positively in general by women than by men (Galvin, 1994, p. 221). For Galvin, this kind of reading is not only alternative, but potentially subversive: 'Women can derive pleasure from not only Catherine's conventional beauty but also her unconventional behaviour – from smoking to wearing no knickers to driving aggressively to sleeping with women to killing men – depending on one's scale of values' (Galvin, 1994, p. 222). Paula Graham notes that protests by the likes of GLAAD all but ignored the representations of women in the film and focused almost exclusively on its alleged homophobic content. She continues, 'Exasperated, one lesbian commentator wryly enquired as to what could be wrong with a film in which women have sex with each other and kill men!' (Graham, 1995, p. 164).

Such oppositional readings of *Basic Instinct* would circumvent the familiar critique of Verhoeven's film that its engagement with female bisexuality works chiefly on the level of an appeal to the familiar male voyeuristic pleasure in 'lipstick lesbianism'. (Eszterhas admitted that his wife believed the movie 'comes out of all my [Eszterhas's] sexual fantasies' (Hoberman, 2005, p. 31)). Lucille Cairns dismisses such images as 'lesbian thrills [that] can become aspirational consumer options *if* their protagonists look just like canonically pretty, straight girls'. As she points out, if they did not, 'they might alienate the boys – and it is the boys who still, by and large, control every aspect of image production' (Cairns, 2006, pp. 6–7).

A number of writers have suggested that *Basic Instinct* offers slim pickings for the heterosexual female viewer. Miranda Sherwin suggests that

Douglas 'has a propensity to star in films that cast him as the object of desire for a beautiful but deadly woman, but Douglas lacks whatever quality it is that makes a star into a sex symbol' (Sherwin, 2008, p. 176). Austin's research reveals that 'The appearance and behaviour of Douglas/Nick was a major cause of dissatisfaction, even among women who enjoyed much of the film' (Austin, 2002, p. 73). Austin concludes that while the male heterosexual viewing pleasure derived primarily from the objectification of the female stars, and a focus on the sex scenes, the female pleasure was located more consistently in the narrative, and the construction of Catherine as 'a sexual and narrative agent' (p. 92), and, presumably, in a celebration of her power and autonomy.

On the other hand, Andrew Spicer notes that it is 'the attractive figure [of] Catherine who offers potential pleasures for women viewers as a strong character with wit and style, enjoying sex and money but not punished for her appetites' (Spicer, 2002, p. 164). This perspective is confirmed by some of the findings of Thomas Austin's audience research, which suggest that responses from female viewers of any sexuality were 'complex and ambivalent, rather than consistently positive or negative' (2002, p. 72). On the one hand, he notes a tendency to dismiss the movie as a 'a very male film', and comments from respondents to the effect that the pleasures for the typical male heterosexual viewer largely derived from the display of Sharon Stone's naked body (pp. 74–6). On the other, he points out that some heterosexual women found Catherine an empowering figure: 'The film could be seen to foreground not just Catherine's body and wardrobe', he points out, '[B]ut also her self-sufficiency, intelligence and aggression – characteristics which appealed to many women' (Austin, 2002, p. 69). Austin noted that 'Several women commented positively on *Basic Instinct*'s representation of female sexual agency and pleasure' ('a rare departure for mainstream film'), and that for some women, straight and bisexual, Catherine actually functioned as 'an advertisement for, or legitimation of, bisexuality and/or lesbianism' (p. 71).

'Just an Old City Cowboy'

It was already being suggested at the time the film was released that it could be read from very different perspectives. Judith Halberstam, having pointed out that *Basic Instinct* 'is a film about women who kill, women who stand up to male aggression, manipulate male sexuality, and refuse to be bullied into some kind of conventional submission', offered a reading of the film that outs Michael Douglas as a lesbian (Halberstam, 1992). The extract below gives a sense of the playful approach to interpretation that Halberstam adopts, centring on costume choices:

> Douglas actually 'comes out' in the movie on the night when he follows Catherine to a dance club. In the club he wears a rather low-cut sweater that shows just enough of his cleavage. The sweater comes off later and Catherine pays serious attention to his small but firm breasts. On the morning after the night before, Michael follows Catherine to her Marin hideout. It is obvious he is feeling vulnerable so he wears his butchest outfit – 501's, a sweater, and a bomber jacket. Later that day, he forces his rival, Roxie [sic], to drive her car off the road and gets ready to replace her as Catherine's lesbian lover.

Halberstam goes on to question Queer Nation's opposition to the film, considering the film 'punishes misogyny and suggests that beneath all heterosexual relations lies a complicated web of sexual relations between women' (Halberstam 1992).

One could just as easily develop a strategy of interpreting the film that turns a spotlight on the relationship between Nick and Gus, which J. Hoberman (1992), Steven Cohan (1998, p. 275) and Celestino Deleyto have read as signifying a repressed homoeroticism. Deleyto notes that, for all the controversy about the film's representation of bisexuality, 'the only same-sex relationship developed in any depth by the film is the one between two men, Nick and Gus' (Deleyto, 1997). Although undoubtedly their relationship lies

in the familiar tradition of cop partnerships, there is still a good deal of scope
for reading between the lines, for anyone so inclined. Nick and Gus hardly
ever use their real names when addressing one another: Gus is 'Cowboy' and
Nick is 'Hoss'. They clearly feel a sense of duty to protect one another:
when Nick starts drinking again, it is Gus who is the first one to challenge
him: 'Whatcha doing, Hoss?', he asks. Nick turns to him and replies, evenly:
'I haven't had a drink in three months. That all right with you, Cowboy?' Later,
when a drunk Gus tries to get in his car to drive home, Nick tries (and fails) to
prevent him. When Nick returns to the office late at night to do some research
on Hazel Dobkins, Gus sidles up and surprises him. 'Haven't you got anything
better to do than come in here and jack off the damn machine?' his partner
asks. 'What are you doing here, Cowboy?' Nick counters. Gus takes a seat and,
in mock confession mode, admits, 'I came in here to jack off the damn
machine.'

   The 'bromance' begins to come apart as Nick becomes increasingly
obsessed with Catherine. Following the morning-after scene, Nick tracks
down Gus in a country-and-western bar, a setting in keeping with their pet
names for one another. Gus, who has been drinking heavily, launches into a
tirade against Nick, asking him where he has been. It does not take Gus very
long – even in his inebriated state – to figure out what Nick's absence from his
apartment signifies: 'You fucked her,' he says, shaking his head in disbelief.
'Goddamn dumb sonofabitch, you fucked her. Goddamn, you are one dumb
sonofabitch.' The conversation breaks down into banter over condoms – 'I'm
worried about him,' Gus mutters to himself, 'and he's worried about *rubbers*' –
and Gus's odd confession about his lack of sexual activity: 'You think I'm
getting any? Sure, I can get laid … by goddamn blue-haired women.' In a
gesture of familiarity, Nick takes Gus's hat and puts it on his own head as they
cross from the bar to a diner, where the conversation continues over sobering
cups of coffee, sounding oddly akin to an exchange between an unfaithful
husband and a jealous wife: 'How could you fuck her?' Gus wants to know.
Still drunk, his voice is raised and attracts the attention of other customers.
Nick is clearly embarrassed ('Gus, come on') but Gus refuses to let up: when

Nick asserts that he is not afraid of Catherine, his friend's loud response provokes even more attention from those seated around them: 'That's her pussy talking,' Gus tells him. 'It ain't your brain.' Deleyto notes that Gus's 'aggressiveness towards her is […] significantly expressed through continuous offensive references to her lethal sexual organ, suggesting the sexual nature of his jealousy and his perception of her as a rival' (Deleyto, 1997). Indeed, the enmity between Gus and Catherine is undisguised, mirroring the Roxy/ Catherine/Nick triangle, perhaps. Gus is aggressively dismissive of Nick's dreams of domestic bliss with Catherine (the 'fuck like minks, raise rugrats, live happily ever after' trope that Nick appropriates for two later conversations with her) and just as Nick removes Catherine's same-sex partner Roxy, so Catherine removes Nick's same-sex partner (while framing Beth for the murder), paving the way for the eventual heterosexual partnering of the hero and heroine at the end of the movie.

The debates that *Basic Instinct* provoked on its release may today seem frozen in another era, at least in terms of cinema spectatorship and cultural consumption more generally. Certainly in terms of identity politics, the furore today seems oddly quaint in some respects. However, precisely because the film-makers insisted on pushing against contemporary boundaries of acceptability in terms of sex, sexuality and violence, it opened up a space for readings that challenged the *status quo*. Catherine may have been, on the one hand, another link in a chain of Hollywood's stereotypical representations of murderous lesbians/bisexuals. On the other, by placing her at the centre of the movie, with a cast of men and women caught helplessly in the web radiating out from her, she represented a new kind of female protagonist, and set down new markers for the *femme fatale* in the Hollywood thriller.

✖ PART 6

THE LEGACY OF *BASIC INSTINCT*

Box Office Risk Addiction

On 26 April 2008, Sharon Stone appeared at the GLAAD annual media awards ceremony, presenting the Stephen F. Kolzak Award to Rufus Wainwright. The Stephen F. Kolzak Award is presented to an openly GLBT media professional who has made a significant difference in promoting equal rights for the GLBT community. Stone was apparently not amused when Wainwright made a move to lift the hem of her dress to check the status of her underwear.

Sixteen years on from *Basic Instinct*, the GLAAD awards had taken on the status of a major event in the Hollywood calendar, and the woman at the centre of the film that had provoked so much revulsion and anger in the gay and lesbian community in 1992 was an honoured guest. Stone has remained a member of Hollywood royalty despite appearing in a generally undistinguished run of films in the time since her breakthrough role. Although there had been a few exceptions, notably her Oscar-nominated and Golden Globe-winning performance in Martin Scorsese's *Casino*, Stone's attempts to escape the legacy of Catherine Tramell had generally been unsuccessful. Talk of a *Basic Instinct* sequel started towards the end of the 1990s, and the film even moved into pre-production in 2000, before collapsing in a flurry of lawsuits. Years of delays, changes of personnel and an out-of-court settlement between Stone and producers Andrew Vajna and Mario Kassar followed. Finally, *Basic Instinct 2: Risk Addiction* was unleashed on the public in April 2006. The public promptly shrugged and turned away. *Basic Instinct 2* grossed only $3.2 million on its opening weekend; the number one slot that week was claimed by *Ice Age: The Meltdown*, on $70.5 million, and Stone's film tied for tenth place with *Larry the Cable Guy: Health Inspector* (*Sun Journal*, 2006). In January 2007, *Basic Instinct 2* would be nominated for seven Golden Raspberry Awards and win four: Worst Actress, Worst Picture, Worst Screenplay and Worst Sequel or Prequel (Germain, 2007). The reviews are not worth dwelling upon. Suffice to say that a website that attempts to provide aggregate scores for all movies by gathering every press and internet review it can gives *Basic Instinct 2* a '7% fresh' score, and ranks it as number 89 in the worst-reviewed movies from 2000–9 (*Larry the Cable Guy: Health Inspector* just pips it at number 85) (rottentomatoes.com, 2009).

Somewhat depressingly, though not surprisingly, much of the attention the film drew, both in marketing and press reaction, centred on Sharon Stone and the challenge not of the role *per se*, but of reprising a performance famed for the (over-)exposure of her naked body at the age of forty-eight. Stone herself was responsible for much of the hype in this respect; interview copy such as, 'I wanted a lot of sex in the sequel, and I wanted more nudity' was typical (Voynar, 2006). In the wake of the film's release, the press punished her mercilessly, punning, parodying and ridiculing her for it; the *New York Daily News* described the film as 'Stone's ode to her body parts' (Diluna, 2006), and this was one of the kinder remarks that made it into print. The entertainment world had changed dramatically in the fourteen-year gap between hit movie and flop sequel, and the publicity campaign built around *Basic Instinct 2* seemed utterly, mystifyingly oblivious to the media and entertainment revolution. By 2006, explicit sex in mainstream film was a rarity and even the market for the direct-to-video 'erotic thriller' had long since collapsed.[33] In an era where everything from hard pornography to 'celebrity skin' was accessible at the click of a mouse, the appeal of Sharon Stone baring all, again, was cause for little more than mild curiosity, and perhaps some nostalgia among those who had enjoyed the marginally illicit thrill of the first movie.

The screenplay of *Basic Instinct 2* has been described by Linda Ruth Williams, somewhat hopefully and very much in the teeth of predominant critical consensus, as 'almost a postmodern parody of an A-list erotic thriller, an occasionally hilarious combination of daft convolution and quick-witted quipping' (Williams, 2006). Undeniably, there are some minor pleasures to be gathered from the wreckage, but one wonders whether they are primarily the decidedly rarefied ones of the academic specialist (Williams remarks upon the '[H]uge scope for Lacanian one-liners, criminal transference and enough phallic symbols to keep academic film analysts going for years' (2006)). As a piece of commercial entertainment, however, the film was generally considered to be dreadful without being quite disastrous enough to be celebrated for its failings in the way that *Showgirls* was.

And what of Michael Douglas? His encounters with dangerous women in the movies culminated with *Disclosure,* in which he played an executive sexually harassed by his boss. Following this, the appeal of such material (either to him, to the industry, or both) seemed to wane. Having gone through the early 1990s trailing rumours of treatment for sex addiction, Douglas settled into a happy second marriage with Catherine Zeta-Jones in 2000. In 2006, the year of *Basic Instinct 2*, he released his last thriller to date (*The Sentinel*), and seemed content to leave both sex and violence behind. He was surprisingly forthcoming about his sense of humiliation when his co-star, Eva Longoria, outran him wearing high heels while filming a chase scene for *The Sentinel* (Londonnet, 2006). Half-jokingly, he indicated how he had ruled himself out of a *Basic Instinct* sequel, self-deprecatingly contrasting Sharon Stone's toned physique with his own physical condition: 'You want to see my saggy ass?', he quipped (Loh, 2010).[34] It is also worthy of note, in relation to the first *Basic Instinct* furore, that in 2002 Douglas took on a special guest-star role playing a gay cop in popular sitcom *Will and Grace* (1998–2006). The episode was called 'Fagel Attraction'. And in 2010, having recovered from stage-four throat cancer, he was happily discussing a forthcoming role as gay icon Liberace in a biopic. 'It's going to be so much fun,' he told one interviewer. 'And part of it is that Matt (Damon) has agreed to play my young lover … God bless him! It's fine for me, at this point in my career. Heck, I'll try anything!' (Loh, 2010).

The Enduring Myth of the Lethal Woman

The *femme fatale*, in her various incarnations, has always been perceived as a potent signifier of female power and as one of the most insidious threats to patriarchy. Janey Place notes that '[t]he dark lady, the spider woman, the evil seductress who tempts man and brings about his destruction is among the oldest themes of art, literature, mythology and religion in Western culture' (Place, 1980, p. 35). Although the term *femme fatale* dates from the early twentieth century, and is most familiar today from the *noir* genre, it is an archetype traceable back to the roots of ancient culture, in Eve tempting Adam to eat from the tree of knowledge and in Pandora, the first woman in Greek mythology, endowed with 'a shameless mind and a deceitful nature' (Allen, 1997, p. 14) and destined to provide nothing but torment to (hu)mankind. Catherine Tramell lies in a direct line of descent from the archetype, one that has remained a staple of art, literature and film, and one that has continued to circulate in culture more widely.

The shadow of Catherine Tramell haunted a number of mainstream films featuring variations on the *femme fatale* in the decade following *Basic Instinct*. Some, such as *Body of Evidence*, I have already noted in passing, and variations on the sexy, dangerous female were a staple of the erotic thriller B-movie genre that mined a lucrative seam in the boom era of home video during the 1990s.[35] A number of more mainstream ventures, meanwhile, took a leaf from Verhoeven's playbook and developed the plan he eventually dropped to exploit the *Basic Instinct* scenario's potentially lucrative lipstick lesbianism. The Wachowski Brothers' *Bound* (1996) was a clever, knowing *noir* featuring relatively explicit sex scenes between ditzy femme Violet (Jennifer Tilly) and vaguely butch Corky (Gina Gershon). In 1998, *Wild Things* starred two young sex symbols, Neve Campbell and Denise Richards, brought together in a threesome with Matt Dillon (the sex scene was largely responsible for the cult attention the film attracted). The following year, *Cruel Intentions* included a scene depicting scheming Catherine's (Sarah Michelle Gellar) attempt to teach her protégée Cecile (Selma Blair) how to French kiss, swiftly becoming another firm favourite among heterosexual men of a certain age.[36]

Sarah Gellar had already established herself playing a very different kind of lethal woman in the popular TV show *Buffy the Vampire Slayer* (1997–2003). It could be argued that the action hero(ine) trope that Joss Whedon's ground-breaking show helped to establish was at least partly responsible for the gradual withdrawal of the traditional *femme fatale* from the scene in the new millennium. *Buffy* stands alongside *Xena: Warrior Princess* (1995–2001), and a number of other TV shows with powerful female protagonists, including *Dark Angel* (2000–2), *Witchblade* (2001–2), *Alias* (2001–6) and *Dollhouse* (2009–10).[37] Early signs of the action heroine may have been discernible on the big screen – Yvonne Tasker refers to the 'musculinity'[38] of the likes of a militarised Sarah Connor in *Terminator 2* and Sigourney Weaver in the *Alien* franchise – but it seems to have been the television medium that first established the trend of the 'kickass', third-wave feminist woman who wasn't afraid of looking glamorous and/or beautiful while establishing equal terms with the male action hero. Cinema picked up on the trend, inevitably, and it currently shows no signs of slowing down. The most notable recent entries include *Wanted* (2008), *Salt* (2010), *Colombiana* (2011) and *Haywire* (2012). In the meantime, more overtly sexualised (and objectified) women combining physical attractiveness and a penchant for violence have cropped up in comic-book sourced fare such as the distastefully misogynist *Sin City* (2005) and the mind-numbing *Sucker Punch* (2011). The jury is still out on precisely where *Kill Bill* (2003–4) fits into the scheme of things.[39]

All these variant forms on the idea of the beautiful, dangerous woman suggest that her allure remains as strong as it ever has been, twenty years after Catherine Tramell so perfectly embodied those patriarchal fears and desires and epitomised the archetype. The *femme fatale* remains a key touchstone when a more or less stable understanding of the world is disrupted by a woman who combines physical charm with uncontrollable violence. Such figures, particularly when they cross over the line between representation and reality, still tend to provoke a particularly conflicted tangle of emotions, including horrified fascination, titillation, stern reproach and damning judgment. Ideological constructions of women such as the *femme fatale,* the Medea-like murderous mother or the monstrous-feminine[40] are very often, and very swiftly, mobilised against women who seem to transgress cultural norms. This study will conclude with a few reflections on one such case that connects in a number of fascinating ways with *Basic Instinct,* and can be seen, however indirectly, as part of the film's legacy.

In 2009, US student Amanda Knox stood trial for her alleged involvement in the murder of the young British woman Meredith Kercher, her fellow student and housemate. Kercher's semi-clothed body had been found on the floor of her bedroom in the house she shared with Knox and two young Italian women, in Perugia, Italy, in November 2007. Kercher had been sexually assaulted and had bled to death from stab wounds to her neck. Within a few days, Knox was arrested on suspicion of murder, along with her Italian boyfriend Raffaele Sollecito. Another suspect, Rudy Guede, was found guilty at a fast-track trial (his bloody handprint had been found near Kercher's body) and sentenced to thirty years in prison in October 2008.[41] Italian prosecutors believed that Kercher was murdered in a drug- and/or alcohol-induced frenzy of sexual violence, at the hands of Knox, Sollecito and Guede. Sollecito and Knox were found guilty in 2009 but acquitted on appeal in 2011, after crucial forensic evidence had been discredited. The combination of the different elements of the story proved irresistible, creating a media storm: two attractive young women, one the victim and one the perpetrator; sex, drugs and alcohol; a bloody, sexualised murder. At the centre of it was a young woman dubbed by the Italian press '*la luciferina*', the devil with an angel's face (Minihan, 2007).

The identification of both Catherine Tramell and Amanda Knox as the devil aside, a survey of some of the early press coverage reveals some striking parallels between their representations. Knox is believed by the prosecutors to have stabbed Meredith Kercher to death in a frenzied knife attack. Further, the prosecutor's version of events implies Knox was involved in a sadomasochistic act that fused murder and rampant sexuality (press reports repeatedly used the phrase 'sex game gone wrong'). The widely reported detail of Knox having written a short story about a violent rape recalls Catherine's habit of enacting the murders she depicts in her books. Just as the investigators in *Basic Instinct* speculate that Catherine's novels might be *romans à clef*, so many reporters and commentators suggested that Knox's story afforded a crucial insight into what had happened that night in Perugia. The salacious potential of lesbian sex is familiar territory for the tabloids; the *Daily Mail* gloried in the headline, 'Foxy Knoxy Claims Female Cell Mate Begs Her for Sex "Because I'm So Pretty"', and the report went on to describe how one of the female guards also propositioned her (Pisa, 2008). There is even a parallel between the questioning of the two women as suspects, although the contrast here is striking. Knox underwent an intensive grilling as the prosecutor Giuliano Mignini and his team sought to determine the extent of her involvement in the crime. However, unlike Catherine, who is never less than fully in control of her interrogation, Knox was at a significant disadvantage, being questioned in a language she had only a passing acquaintance with. She claims to have been bullied into signing a statement (in Italian) in which she admitted to having been present at the crime scene.[42] Her accusations that she was struck on the head several times are the subject of an ongoing court case at the time of writing. Finally, in one of the most bizarre reports of all, the *Sun* concocted a story with the headline, 'Knox Had "No Pants On in Jail"', thus managing to draw a direct line between her and one of the most famous scenes in Hollywood history (*Sun*, 2008).

There is an element of playfulness, of course, in 'reading' the Amanda Knox case via *Basic Instinct*, but it is revealing on a number of counts: in the first place, and most obviously, it illuminates certain value judgments that were in play in the press coverage of Knox's trial to do with sexuality, and the idea (or the fantasy) of a young woman engaged in a brutal act of violence. Second, it underlines the significance of authorship and autonomy. The amount of control these women are able to exert over the stories told about themselves starkly illuminates the issues of power that are at stake. As I

Figure 19: Catherine Tramell.

noted in Part 5 (see pp. 115–18), Tramell's frank language and unashamed
attitude in the assertion of her right to sexual pleasure shocks her male
interrogators. By allowing her to parade her sexual autonomy, her
transgressive nature and behaviour (sex, drugs), her lack of shame with
regard to those transgressions, and her potential for danger (is she or is she
not the killer?), the men who inadvertently expose their conflicted response
– indignation and sexual desire – to full view.

     Press coverage of Amanda Knox reveals a similar process, a
simultaneous reaction of disgust at the idea of a young, attractive woman
involved in a brutal murder – worse, the murder of another woman – and, on
the other hand, a lurid fascination with Knox's supposed sexual depravity.
Headline reports frequently refer to Amanda by a nickname her family
claimed she earned as a child on the football field, 'Foxy Knoxy'. The Italian
press (Knox was voted woman of the year there in 2008) called her 'the Dark
Lady of Seattle', and *una cacciatrice d'uomini, insaziabile a letto* (a huntress of

Figure 20: Amanda Knox.

men, insatiable in bed) (*Corriere della Sera*, 2007). One of the prosecuting lawyers referred to her as a 'she-devil', a term that the press picked up on and deployed repeatedly in their headlines (Pisa, 2011). In the words of one reporter, 'If Kercher was seen as the virginal ingenue victimized by this horrendous crime, Knox was immediately cast as its heartless, sexually voracious villain' (Horne, 2008). Like Catherine Tramell, unashamed to admit she prioritises her own pleasure, Knox is reported to have been described by her lover Sollecito as a hedonist: 'She [Amanda] lived life like a dream, reality didn't enter. Her only goal was the search for pleasure at all times' (Moore, 2007). Journals leaked from Knox's cell have been routinely described as 'sex diaries' by tabloid reporters, with all kinds of claims about her sexual exploits and multiple partners. Some of the higher-brow press coverage sought to raise the tone of the debate, only to catch Knox in a curious double-bind:

> Her diaries have been leaked to the press and are minutely scrutinised for evidence of sexual deviancy. It is all prurient and intrusive but by no means irrelevant. For the question of Ms Knox's sexual appetites, and how far she will go to gratify them, go to the heart of this disturbing case. (Popham, 2009)

The focus on her appetites – that they are an issue is not in question, only the extent of them, apparently – is bound up in the image of Amanda Knox circulated in the media as the trial continued: repeatedly depicted as a young woman out of control, transgressing accepted boundaries of female decency, pursuing her appetite for drink, drugs and sex in the liberated, limbo status of a student on a year abroad. Neither was this kind of discourse limited to the press. The judges' justification of their decision to keep Amanda in jail until her trial was underpinned by a claim that she had '*una multiforme personalità*' – a multifaceted personality, 'composed of both self-possession and cunning … and a heightened – one might say fatal – capacity for manipulation' (Bachrach, 2008). One can almost hear the echo of Dr Lamott's horrified tone as he offers his diagnosis of Catherine Tramell's 'devious, diabolical mind'.

In *Basic Instinct,* part of Tramell's alibi is that she would hardly have written novels about murder and then gone on to commit those crimes in real life, since she would have been announcing herself as the killer. Of course, it's a double bluff: Tramell is the killer, but the bluff works, and everyone except Nick is convinced of her innocence. Knox was less fortunate. Her own foray into creative writing was a story about a rape, written as a class assignment and then posted on her MySpace website, where it was found by investigative reporters. There was no alibi here, no 'advance defence mechanism', as Lamott fussily describes Catherine's strategy of constructing her own alibi: in classic intentional-fallacy mode, Knox's story was eagerly interpreted as a key to understanding her behaviour on that night in Perugia.[43] Unlike the fantasy figure Catherine Tramell, scripting roles for men and women alike and watching them running in circles around her, Knox, having authored a version of herself, had no control over the Amandas fashioned out of her social-networking pages.[44] Knox's virtual identities, and her haplessly published diaries, were up for grabs, available to anyone who wished to construct their own dramas out of the raw material, dramas that are conditioned by these bizarrely opposite, but mutually attracting forces: an outraged sense of decency and salacious fascination.

In the fantasy space of the Hollywood erotic thriller, Catherine Tramell sweeps all before her. Her power resides not solely in her capacity to determine her own fate, but in the control she exerts over others: she essentially writes herself and those around her a narrative, managing to get away with murder several times by scripting the roles and actions of those she comes into contact with, framing an innocent woman for the killings and escaping to enjoy (yet another) enthusiastic sex scene in the final sequence with the cop who had been investigating her, while keeping her ice-pick handy under the bed. Furthermore, she deploys herself in a number of different roles – ice queen/red-hot lover, vulnerable victim/vicious killer, straight/lesbian – which in effect render her essentially unknowable – certainly for the cop on her trail, if not for the audience. It is by keeping her identity in flux that Catherine is able to avoid attempts by the police to pin her definitively to the murders. However, it also leaves her firmly located in the realm of Hollywood's imagination, where she remains (for audiences) a thrill-inducing, but safely sheathed figure, neatly wrapped up in several layers of fantasy. For the writers poring over Knox's story, the fragments of her personality, real, fictional and aspirational, come together, with a dreadful inevitability, to form the familiar shape of the archetypal *femme fatale*.

Does a figure like Catherine reaffirm old stereotypes by fusing a murderous psychopathology with 'deviant' sexuality? Does she then in turn recirculate those myths about female sexuality, deviousness and violence? Or is there a more progressive way to interpret her? Judith Halberstam suggests that 'the power of fantasy is not to represent but to destabilize the real', and evokes what she terms 'imagined violence' in the field of cultural representations, i.e. 'the fantasy of unsanctioned eruptions of aggression from "the wrong people, of the wrong skin, the wrong sexuality, the wrong gender"'. She argues that while 'Imagined violence does not advocate lesbian or female aggression,' nevertheless 'it might complicate an assumed relationship between women and passivity or feminism and pacifism.' In this way, she believes, 'imagined violences challenge white powerful heterosexual masculinity and create a cultural coalition of postmodern terror' (Halberstam, 1993, p. 199).

With the GLAAD-style response to *Basic Instinct* now largely of historical interest, the film's enduring significance in terms of controversy perhaps inheres in this: the ways in which we choose to interpret the *femme fatale*'s ambiguous qualities in ideological terms. Despite (or, rather, because of) her roots in male fear and fantasy, Catherine can take on the role of stereotype, a reflex reaction to the threat of the deviant female. Alternatively, we may choose to read her as a a powerfully subversive signifier, a challenge to the complacent values of a society still too ready to reassert traditional values and gender roles.

✖ APPENDICES

Appendix A: Key Details

Cast

Nick Curran	Michael Douglas	Hazel Dobkins	Dorothy Malone
Catherine Tramell	Sharon Stone	John Corelli	Wayne Knight
Gus	George Dzundza	Marty Nilsen	Daniel von Bargen
Beth Garner	Jeanne Tripplehorn	Dr Lamott	Stephen Tobolowsky
Lieutenant Walker	Denis Arndt	Harrigan	Benjamin Mouton
Roxy	Leilani Sarelle	Sheriff	Jack McGee
Andrews	Bruce A. Young	Johnny Boz	Bill Cable
Captain Talcott	Chelcie Ross		

Production Crew

Director	Paul Verhoeven	Special Make-up Effects	Rob Bottin
Producer	Alan Marshall	Original Music	Jerry Goldsmith
Written by	Joe Eszterhas	Costume Designer	Ellen Mirojnick
Executive Producer	Mario Kassar	Associate Producers	William S. Beasley
Director of Photography	Jan de Bont, A.S.C.		Louis D'Esposito
Production Designer	Terence Marsh		Nina Kostroff
Editor	Frank J. Urioste, A.C.E.	Casting	Howard Feuer

Other Details

Filmed at Warner Brothers Burbank Studios and on location in San Francisco, Big Sur, Carmel Highlands and Carmel Valley, San Rafael, Oakland and Petaluma, California. Shooting commenced 5 April 1991 and finished 10 September 1991.

Released
20 March 1992 (US), 8 May 1992 (UK).

Budget
Estimated $40 million.
Opening Weekend: $ 15 million (approx.).
Gross: $235 million worldwide (excluding US). 117.7 million (US).

Awards
Nominated for Palme d'Or 1992 (Jerry Goldsmith).
Nominated for Academy Awards 1993: Best Film Editing (Frank J. Urioste); Best Music, Original Score (Jerry Goldsmith).
Won BMI Film Music Award 1993 (Jerry Goldsmith).
Nominated for Golden Globes 1993: Best Original Score – Motion Picture (Jerry Goldsmith); Best Performance by an Actress in a Motion Picture – Drama (Sharon Stone).
Nominated for MTV Movie Awards 1993: Best Male Performance (Michael Douglas); Best Movie. Won MTV Movie Awards Best Female Performance (Sharon Stone); Most Desirable Female (Sharon Stone).
Nominated for Razzie Awards 1993: Worst Actor (Michael Douglas, also nominated in the same year for *Shining Through*); Worst Supporting Actress (Jeanne Tripplehorn); Worst New Star ('Sharon Stone's "Tribute to Theodore Cleaver"').

Certification and Ratings
Argentina: 18
Australia: R (18+)
Belgium: KNT (16+)
Brazil: 18
Canada: R (18+)
Canada (Quebec): 16+ (re-rating) (same applies to director's cut)
Chile: 18
Finland: K-18 (theatrical); K-16 (video; cut)
France: 16 (theatrical); 12 (re-rating)
Germany: 16
Hong Kong: III (18+)
Hungary: 18
Iceland: 16
India: A (Adults only: 18+)
Ireland: 18
Israel: X (theatrical); 18 (video)
Italy: VM14

Malaysia: Banned
Netherlands: 16
New Zealand: R18
Norway: 18 (theatrical); 15 (video)
Peru: 18
Philippines: R
Portugal: M/18
Singapore: R (A) (*cut*) (1992); PG (video rating; heavily cut); R21 (re-rating)
Spain: 18
Sweden: 15
UK: 18
USA: R; Unrated (director's cut)[45]

Appendix B: Notes

1 To whom the real credit belongs for the original idea remains a disputed question – see pp. 15–17.

2 I am very grateful to Edward Lamberti and others at the BBFC for allowing me access to the file on *Basic Instinct* held at the Board's archive.

3 In his collection of reflections and *bons mots*, *The Devil's Guide to Hollywood* (2007), Eszterhas claims to have written the screenplay in ten days (p. 203).

4 Elsewhere, Verhoeven has, more straightforwardly, described *Basic Instinct* as an 'Americanization' of his earlier film (Bouineau, 2001, p. 91).

5 The quotation comes from the film's Final Production Notes, from its publicity pack, sourced from BBFC files (p. 24).

6 See the Region 2 10th Anniversary Special Edition (2002) and the Region 1 Ultimate Edition (2006).

7 Available on a number of DVD editions, including the US Unrated Collector's Edition (2001), US Special Edition (2003), US Ultimate Edition (Unrated Director's Cut) (2006) and the UK 10th Anniversary Special Edition (2002).

8 For further discussion, see Jones (2006).

9 The events are dramatised in the 2009 movie *Milk*, starring Sean Penn in the title role. Milk and Moscone's killer, Dan White, was found guilty only of voluntary manslaughter on the grounds of diminished responsibility due to depression. The so-called White Night riots that followed are the subject of Chuck Prophet's song *White Night, Big City* on the album *Temple Beautiful* (Yep Roc, 2012). Following the riots, Harry Britt, who had replaced Milk as supervisor, declared that 'Harvey Milk's people do not have anything to apologize for. Now the society is going to have to deal with us not as nice little fairies who have hairdressing salons, but as people capable of violence' (jointheimpact.com, 2009). Britt would be a key figure in the negotiations over the script of *Basic Instinct* in the summit meeting between the production team and protest-group leaders (see pp. 32–4).

10 It should be noted that this is a misrepresentation of the scene, which ends with Beth angry and dismissive.

11 Speaking on the documentary *Blonde Poison*, included on various DVD editions of the film: see note 7.

12 From the *Blonde Poison* documentary.

13 Commentary included on various DVD editions; see note 7.

14 See especially pp. 99–105.

15 Named after George Moscone: see footnote 9.

16 The Golden Raspberry Award Foundation was established in 1980 to celebrate the worst Hollywood movies each year in a kind of alternative Academy Awards.

17 It should also be noted that *Basic Instinct* was nominated for three Razzies: Michael Douglas for Worst Actor, Jeanne Tripplehorn for Worst Supporting Actress and 'Sharon Stone's tribute to Theodore Cleaver' (i.e. her vagina) for Worst New Star.

18 Taken from Hollywood film script repository at http://corky.net/scripts/basicInstinct.html, accessed online 15 February 2012.

19 On the DVD commentary, Verhoeven says that it is not possible to tell from the film as shot whether the act is anal sex or rear entry.

20 Director of Photography Jan de Bont notes that this signifies 'he is in her prison right now' (commentary track).

21 Unless otherwise noted, details of the BBFC's treatment of the film come from the BBFC's file on *Basic Instinct* held at the BBFC archive.

22 I can find no record of any cuts to *Jagged Edge* in the BBFC's database, or in its BBFC file.

23 Letter dated 18 May 1992, from the BBFC file.

24 Letter dated 17 June 1992, from the BBFC file.

25 Letter dated 10 August 1992, from the BBFC file.

26 The saga is covered in great detail by Julian Petley in his *Film and Video Censorship in Modern Britain* (2011).

27 Queer Nation media coordinator Rich Wilson, quoted in Lyons (1997, p. 134).

28 Director Jonathan Demme's next project would be *Philadelphia* (1994), an AIDS drama with a gay lawyer as the protagonist; the role was taken by Tom Hanks, who would win an Oscar for it.

29 *Truth or Dare*, released in the UK under the title *In Bed with Madonna,* included a number of scenes featuring gay and bisexual friends and associates of Madonna who were depicted without drawing attention to their sexuality as anything out of the ordinary.

30 According to a report in *Time* magazine, Oliver Stone would abandon plans for a biopic of Harvey Milk in the wake of threats by Queer Nation to picket the set, in retaliation for what they saw as negative representations of gay characters in previous films (notably *JFK*) (Simpson, 1992, p. 65).

31 DVD commentary track.

32 Paul Verhoeven and Jan de Bont discuss this at some length on the DVD commentary track.

33 See Linda Ruth Williams (2005), especially the Introduction and the interview with direct-to-video erotic thriller producers Andrew Garroni and Walter Gernert (pp. 1–73).

34 By this time, the tabloids were wallowing in headlines such as, 'I Have to Take Viagra to Keep up with Catherine Zeta-Jones: Michael Douglas, 65, Reveals Their Bedroom Secrets' (*Daily Mail*, 2010).

35 See extensive discussion in Williams (2005).

36 *Cruel Intentions* recast de Laclos' eighteenth-century novel *Les Liaisons Dangereuses* in a US college context. The story had already been adapted for the screen in its original period setting: *Dangerous Liaisons* (1988) had featured Glenn Close as the scheming Marquise de Merteuil. It was her next film after *Fatal Attraction*.

37 The scholarly literature on the genre is extensive. See, for example, Inness (1999 and 2004), Kaveney (2001), Wilcox and Lavery (2002), Wilcox (2005), Levine and Parks (2007), Johnson (2007), and the *Slayage* website (http://slayageonline.com/, accessed online 23 March 2012).

38 See Yvonne Tasker (1993), especially pp. 32–52.

39 See for example Anderson (2005), Simkin (2005), pp. 216–19, Smeli (2007) and Waites (2008).

40 See Creed (1993).

41 A cultural stereotype of a different kind circulated early in the investigation. During questioning, Knox falsely accused a Congolese bar owner, Patrick Lumumba, of killing Meredith Kercher, and he was held by the authorities until his alibi was established. Guede was originally from the Ivory Coast. The assumptions that might be at work here (Knox's, the authorities', the journalists' in their press coverage) raise difficult questions about attitudes towards race.

42 Knox would later retract the statement.

43 My interest here is in the media representation of Amanda Knox, not her guilt or innocence with regard to the murder, a crime of which she was first convicted and later acquitted. At the time of writing, the prosecution is preparing to appeal against the acquittal.

44 It should be noted that some of the uncertainty around the truth of what happened that night, in the wake of the acquittal of Knox and Sollecito, lingers as a result of the conflicting stories Knox herself provided. In a witness statement given on 2 November 2007, Knox claimed to have spent the whole night at Sollecito's apartment; on 6 November, she claimed to have been in the kitchen at the flat she shared with Kercher, and added that she heard Meredith's screams when Lumumba attacked her; this was substantiated by a voluntary handwritten note the same day, which she commented at the time was 'the best truth I have been able to think' (cited in Nadeau, 2010, p. 75); in court testimony in June 2009, she reverted to her original story that she had spent the night at Sollecito's.

45 Cast and crew details taken from press release; other details adapted from imdb.com, accessed online 30 March 2012 at http://www.imdb.com/title/tt0103772/maindetails.

Appendix C: References

Alcorn, Keith (1991) 'Split Screen', *Guardian*, 24 July, p. 17.

Allen, Prudence (1997) *The Concept of Woman: the Aristotelian Revolution, 750 BC–AD 1250*. Cambridge: Wm. B. Eerdmans Publishing Company.

Anderson, Aaron (2005) 'Mindful Violence: The Visibility of Power and Inner Life in *Kill Bill*', *Jump Cut* vol. 47, Winter. Accessed online 25 March 2012 at http://www.ejumpcut.org/archive/jc47.2005/KillBill/index.html.

Anderson, George (1992) '*Basic Instinct* Slick and Mean', *Pittsburgh Post-Gazette*, 20 March, p. 3.

Appiah, K. Anthony (1993) '"No Bad Nigger": Blacks as the Ethical Principle in the Movies', in Marjorie Garber *et al.* (eds), *Media Spectacles*. New York and London: Routledge, pp. 77–90.

Austin, Thomas (1999) '"Desperate to See It": Straight Men Watching *Basic Instinct*', in Melvyn Stokes and Richard Maltby (eds), *Identifying Hollywood's Audiences: Cultural Identity and the Movies*. London: BFI.

Austin, Thomas (2002) *Hollywood, Hype and Audiences: Selling and Watching Popular Film in the 1990s*. Manchester: Manchester University Press.

Bachrach, Judy (2008) 'Perugia's Prime Suspect', *Vanity Fair*, 12 May, accessed online 26 February 2012 at http://www.vanityfair.com/culture/features/2008/06/perugia200806?currentPage=5.

Banner, Simon (1992) 'Hype, Gore and a Hit Film That Appeals to Basic Instincts', *Evening Standard*, 27 March, p. 17.

BBFC (1993) *BBFC Annual Report for 1992*, July. London: British Board of Film Classification.

BBFC (2000) *BBFC Classification Guidelines*, September. London: British Board of Film Classification.

Bell, Arthur (1979) 'Bell Tells', *Village Voice*, 16 July.

Benshoff, Harry M. and Sean Griffin (2004) *Queer Cinema: The Film Reader*. London: Routledge.

Bergson, Philip (1992) 'The Ice-pick Cometh', *What's on in London*, 27 May, pp. 4–5.

Bonfante, Jordan (1992) 'Whatever Became of NC-17?', *Time* vol. 139 no. 4, p. 64.

Bouineau, Jean-Marc (2001) *Paul Verhoeven: Beyond Flesh and Blood*. Paris: Cinéditions.

Bould, Mark, Kathrina Glitre and Greg Tuck (2009) 'Parallax Views: An Introduction', in Bould, Glitre and Tuck (eds), *Neo-Noir*. London: Wallflower Press.

Bouzereau, Laurent (1994) *Cutting Room Floor: Movie Scenes Which Never Made It to the Screen*. New York: Citadel Press.

Boxofficemojo.com (2012a) 'Color of Night', accessed online 13 February 2012 at http://boxofficemojo.com/movies/?id=colorofnight.htm.

Boxofficemojo.com (2012b) 'Body of Evidence', accessed online 13 February 2012 at http://boxofficemojo.com/movies/?id=bodyofevidence.htm.

Brown, Geoff (1992) 'Body Count at Maximum', *Times*, 7 May.

Cairns, Lucille (2006) *Sapphism on Screen: Lesbian Desire in French and Francophone Cinema*. Edinburgh: Edinburgh University Press.

City Limits (1992) 'Basic Instinct', 7 May, p. 25.

Coffey, Irene (1992) 'Basic Instinct', *Spare Rib*, June, p. 20.

Cohan, Steven (1998) 'Censorship and Narrative Indeterminacy in *Basic Instinct*: "You Won't Learn Anything from Me I don't Want You to Know"', in Steve Neale and Murray Smith (eds), *Contemporary Hollywood Cinema*. London and New York: Routledge.

Corriere della Sera (2007) 'Amanda voleva solo sesso', 25 November 2007, accessed online 13 July 2010 at http://www.corriere.it/cronache/07_novembre_25/amanda_cacciatrice_uomini_00229488-9b60-11dc-8d30-0003ba99c53b.shtml.

Cox, Peter (1992) 'Douglas Earns His Strips', *Sun*, 8 May, p. 15.

Creed, Barbara (1993) *The Monstrous-feminine: Film, Feminism, Psychoanalysis*. London: Routledge.

Daily Mail (1991) 'Sharon Strips for Action', 15 February, p. 23.

Daily Mail (1995) 'Video Led to Knife Attack', 18 August, p. 33.

Daily Mail (2010) 'I Have to Take Viagra to Keep up with Catherine Zeta-Jones: Michael Douglas, 65, Reveals Their Bedroom Secrets', *Mailonline*, 23 January, accessed online 25 February 2012 at http://www.dailymail.co.uk/ tvshowbiz/article-1245279/Michael-Douglas-admits-I-Viagra-Catherine-Zeta-Jones.html.

Davenport, Hugo (1992) 'A Basic Instinct for Big Profits', *Daily Telegraph*, 7 May, p. 14.

Davies, Jude and Carol R. Smith (1997) *Gender, Ethnicity and Sexuality in Contemporary American Film*. Edinburgh: Keele University Press.

Deleyto, Celestino (1997) 'The Margins of Pleasure: Female Monstrosity and Male Paranoia in "Basic Instinct"', *Film Criticism* vol. 21 no. 3, Spring. Accessed online 17 December 2008 at http://www. americanpopularculture.com/journal/articles/fall_2009/cragin.htm.

Derry, Charles (1988) *The Suspense Thriller: Films in the Shadow of Alfred Hitchcock* Jefferson, NC and London: McFarland & Company, Inc.

Diluna, Amy (2006) 'She's Sharon Too Much. Stone Trusts "Instinct", but Risks Overexposure', *New York Daily News*, 31 March, accessed online 25 February 2012 at http://articles.nydailynews.com/2006-03-31/entertainment/18334438_1_sharon-stone-hot-tub-button-down.

DiNicola, Dan (1992) 'Sexually Charged "Basic Instinct" Has Lot to Offer Despite Controversy', *Daily Gazette*, 26 March, p. D5.

Dudek, Duane (1992) ' "Basic Instinct" Glorifies Violence', *Milwaukee Sentinel*, 20 March, p. 3D.

Earle, Laurence (1992) 'Basic Instinct', 8 May, p. 18.

Ebert, Roger (1992) 'Basic Instinct', *Chicago Sun-Times*, 20 March. Accessed online 23 December 2011 at http://rogerebert.suntimes.com/apps/pbcs.dll/article?AID=/19920320/REVIEWS/203200301/1023.

Ellicott, Susan (1992) 'Total Recoil – *Basic Instinct* ', *Sunday Times*, 22 March, accessed online 10 February 2009 via www.infoweb.newsbank.com.

Empire (1992) 'It's Only a Movie', no. 35, May, p. 6.

Entertainment Weekly (1992) 'Back to "Basic"', 22 May, no. 119, p. 56.

Erhart, Julia (2004) 'Laura Mulvey Meets Catherine Tramell Meets the She-Man: Counter-history, Reclamation, and Incongruity in Lesbian, Gay, and Queer Film and Media Criticism', in Toby Miller and Robert Stam (eds), *A Companion to Film Theory*. Oxford: Blackwell Publishing Ltd, pp. 165–81.

Erickson, Todd (1996) 'Kill Me Again: Movement Becomes Genre', in Alain Silver and James Ursini (eds), *Film Noir Reader*. New York: Limelight Editions, pp. 307–29.

Eszterhas, Joe (2005) *Hollywood Animal*. London: Arrow Books.

Eszterhas, Joe (2007) *The Devil's Guide to Hollywood: The Screenwriter as God*. London: Gerald Duckworth & Co.

Faludi, Susan (1993) *Backlash: The Undeclared War against Women*. London: Vintage.

Feasey, Rebecca (2003) 'Sex, Controversy, Box Office: From Blockbuster to Bonkbuster', in Julian Stringer (ed.), *Movie Blockbusters*. London: Routledge, pp. 167–77.

Fetner, Tina (2008) *How the Religious Right Shaped Lesbian and Gay Activism*. Minneapolis: University of Minnesota Press.

Fox, David J. and Donna Rosenthal (1991) 'Gays Bashing "Basic Instinct"', *Los Angeles Times*, 29 April, accessed online 16 October 2008 at http://www.toobeautiful.org/lat0429.html.

French, Philip (1992) 'Basic Instinct', *Observer*, 10 May, p. 52.

Galvin, Angela (1994) '*Basic Instinct*: Damning Dykes' Cinema', in Diane Hamer and Belinda Budge (eds), *The Good, the Bad and the Gorgeous*. London: Pandora, pp. 218–31.

Garey, Juliann (1992) 'Kiss and Makeup', *Entertainment Weekly* no. 110, 20 March, p. 50.

Gay Times (1992) *Basic Instinct* review, May, p. 69.

Germain, David (2007) '"Instinct 2", Stone Top Razzies as Year's Worst', *Boston Globe*, 28 February, accessed online 25 February 2012 at http://articles.boston.com/2007-02-26/ae/29230485_1_worst-prequel-or-sequel-razzies-filmmaker-m-night-shyamalan.

GLAAD archive (undated) Cultural Media Interest Project, Bisexual Representations, accessed online 17 February 2012 at http://archive.glaad.org/programs/cim/ birepresentations.php.

Gleiberman, Owen (1992) 'Basic Instinct', *Entertainment Weekly* no. 110, 20 March, p. 50.

Goldstein, Richard (1992) *Village Voice*, 14 April.

Goodman, Mark (1992) 'Basic Instinct', *People Weekly* vol. 37 no. 12, 30 March, p. 17.

Graham, Paula (1995) 'Girl's Camp? The Politics of Parody', in Tamsin Wilton (ed.), *Immortal Invisible: Lesbians and the Moving Image*. London and New York: Routledge, pp. 163–81.

Greig, Geordie (1992) 'Too Hot to Handle', *Sunday Times*, 26 January, Section 6, p. 13.

Grist, Leighton (1992) 'Moving Targets and Black Widows: Film Noir in Modern Hollywood', in Ian Cameron (ed.), *The Movie Book of Film Noir*. London: Studio Vista/Cassell, pp. 267–85.

Halberstam, Judith (1992) *Basic Instinct*, accessed online 2 Deccember 2008 at http://www.planetout.com/popcornq/db/getfilm.html?1897.

Halberstam, Judith (1993) 'Imagined Violence/Queer Violence: Representation, Rage, and Resistance', *Social Text* no. 37, Winter, pp. 187–201.

Hamby, Amanda (1992) 'Controversy Bypassed Area', *TimesDaily*, 20 April, p. 10E.

Harris, Scott and Miles Corwin (1992) 'Opposition to Film "Basic Instinct" Rises', *Los Angeles Times*, 21 March, accessed online 15 February 2012 at http://articles.latimes. com/1992-03-21/local/me-3817_1_basic-instinct.

Hoberman, J. (1992) 'Blood Libel', *Village Voice*, 31 March, p. 55.

Hoberman, J. (2005) '*Basic Instinct*: A Geyser of Pathology', in Jamie Bernard (ed.), *The X List: The National Society of Film Critics' Guide to the Movies That Turn Us On*. New York: Da Capo Press.

Horn, John (1992) 'Activists: "Basic Instinct" Basic Homophobia', *Free Lance-Star*, 19 March, p. A5.

Horne, Sarah (2008) 'The Accused', October/November, accessed online 12 January 2009 at http://www.radaronline.com/from-the-magazine/2008/10/amanda_knox_trial_meredith_ kercher_murder_rudy_guede_raffael_sollecito_01-print.php.

Howe, Desson (1992) 'Basic Instinct', *Washington Post*, 20 March, accessed online 22 December 2011 at http://www.washingtonpost.com/wp-srv/style/longterm/movies/videos/basicinstinctrhowe_a0aeaf.htm.

Hughes, Anthony D. (2008) 'Fashionable *Femme Fatales:* Cutting the Edges of Customary Morality in Verhoeven's *Basic Instinct'*, in Anthony D. Hughes *et al*. (eds), *Modern and Postmodern Cutting Edge Films*. Cambridge: Cambridge Scholars Publishing.

Independent (1992) 12 June, p. 16.

Inness, Sherrie A. (1999) *Tough Girls: Women Warriors and Wonder Women in Popular Culture*. Philadelphia: University of Pennsylvania Press.

Inness, Sherrie A. (2004) *Action Chicks: New Images of Tough Women in Popular Culture*. Basingstoke: Palgrave Macmillan.

Johnson, Brian D. and V. Dwyer (1992) 'Killer Movies', *Maclean's* vol. 105 no. 13, 30 March, pp. 48–51.

Johnson, Merri Lisa (2007) *Third Wave Feminism: Jane Puts It in a Box*. London: I. B. Tauris.

jointheimpact.com (2009) 'Our History: White Night Riots', 21 May, accessed online 27 February 2012 at http://jointheimpact.com/2009/05/our-history-white-night-riots/.

Jones, Amy Tilton (2006) 'George Bush and the Religious Right', in Martin J. Medhurst (ed.), *The Rhetorical Presidency of George H. W. Bush*. College Station, TX: A & M University Press, pp. 149–70.

Kauffman, L. A. (1992) 'Queer Guerrillas in Tinseltown', *Progressive* vol. 56 no. 7, July, pp. 36–7.

Kaveney, Roz (ed.) (2001) *Reading the Vampire Slayer: An Unofficial Critical Companion to Buffy and Angel*. London: I. B. Tauris.

Keesey, Douglas and Paul Duncan (eds) (2005) *Paul Verhoeven*. Cologne: Taschen Books.

Kempley, Rita (1992) 'Basic Instinct', *Washington Post*, 20 March, accessed online 22 December 2011 at http://www.washingtonpost.com/wp-srv/style/longterm/movies/videos/basicinstinctrkempley_a0a2a8.htm.

King, Neal (2004) 'Spinning Misogyny: Filmmaker Defenses against Charges of Deviance', Annual Meeting of the Society for Cinema and Media Studies, Atlanta, March. Accessed online 22 December 2011 at http://www.allacademic.com/meta/p_mla_apa_research_citation/1/1/0/1/3/p110136_index.html.

Knewstubb, Nikki (1995) 'Housewife "Acted Out Film Stabbing"', *Guardian*, 18 August.

Lane, Anthony (1992) 'Basic Instinct', *Independent on Sunday*, 10 May, p. 18.

Leo, John (1992) 'The Politics of Intimidation', *US News and World Report* vol. 112 no. 13, 6 April, p. 24.

Letts, Vanessa (1992) 'Base Instinct', *Spectator*, 16 May, pp. 36–7.

Levine, Elana and Lisa Parks (eds) (2007) *Undead TV: Essays on Buffy the Vampire Slayer*. Durham, NC: Duke University Press.

Lew, Julie (1991) 'Gay Groups Protest a Film Script', *New York Times*, 4 May, accessed online October 4 2008 at http://query.nytimes.com/gst/fullpage.html?res=9D0CE7D6153CF937A35756C0A967958260&sec=&spon=&pagewanted=all#.

Lewis, Jon (2000) *Hollywood v. Hard Core: How the Struggle over Censorship Saved the Modern Film Industry*. New York: NYU Press.

Loh, Genevieve (2010) 'The Man's Still Got It', channelnewsasia.com, 22 September, accessed online 25 February 2012 at http://www.channelnewsasia.com/stories/moviesfeatures/view/1082668/1/.html.

Londonnet (2006) 'Michael Douglas Says He's Getting Too Old for Action Films', 29 December, accessed online 26 February 2012 at http://www.londonnet.co.uk/entertainment/2006/dec/4411_20061229.php.

Lovell, Glenn (1992) '"Basic Instinct" Gives New Meaning to "Fatale"', *Spokane Chronicle*, 20 March, p. 14.

Lyons, Charles (1997) *The New Censors: Movies and the Culture Wars*. Philadelphia, PA: Temple University Press.

McClellan, J. (1992), 'Psycho Drama', *Face*, May, pp. 89–92.

McGregor, Alex (1992) 'Sex Crimes', *Time Out*, 22 April, pp. 18–21.

McIlheney, Barry (1992) 'Basic Instinct', *Empire*, Issue 36, June, p. 20.

McNary, Dave (1990) 'Hollywood Writers Getting Bigger Piece of the Pie', *Daily Gazette*, 11 July, p. C6.

Maher, Kathleen (1992) 'Basic Instinct', *Austin Chronicle*, 27 March, accessed online 22 December 2011 at http://www.austinchronicle.com/calendar/film/1992-03-27/138836/.

Mars-Jones, Adam (1992) 'Mad, Bad and Dangerous to Know', *Independent*, 8 May, p. 18.

Marx, Andy (1992) 'We Thought about It (Really) and Decided That Movie Endings Are Special', *Los Angeles Times*, 16 February, accessed 12 February 2012 online at http://articles.latimes.com/1992-02-16/entertainment/ca-4656_1_movie-endings.

Maslin, Janet (1992a) 'Sure, She May Be Mean, But Is She a Murderer?', 20 March 1992, accessed 14 December 2011 online at http://movies.nytimes.com/movie/review?res=9E0CE7DE1F3DF933A15750C0A964958260.

Maslin, Janet (1992b) 'This Year's Cannes Film Festival Somewhat Peculiar from the Start', *Spokesman-Review*, 12 May, p. F9.

Metro.co.uk (2011) 'Sharon Stone's Basic Instinct Leg-crossing Scene Most Paused in Movie History', 23 February, accessed online 29 February 2012 at http://www.metro.co.uk/film/856399-sharon-stones-basic-instinct-leg-crossing-scene-most-paused-in-movie-history.

Minihan, Mary (2007) 'The Girl Italians Are Calling Luciferina – with the Face of an Angel', *Independent.ie*, accessed online 29 March 2012 at http://www.independent.ie/world-news/the-girl-italians-are-calling-luciferina-with-the-face-of-an-angel-1241387.html.

Moodie, Clemmie (2007) '"My Fatal Attraction Role Rescued Marriages", claims Glenn Close', 27 December, accessed online 5 December 2008 at http://www.dailymail.co.uk/tvshowbiz/article-504787/My-Fatal-Attraction-role-rescued-marriages-claims-Glenn-Close.html.

Moore, Malcolm (2007) 'Knox "a Fantasist", Says Meredith Suspect', *Daily Telegraph*, 24 November, accessed online 26 February 2012 at http://www.telegraph.co.uk/news/worldnews/1570389/Knox-a-fantasist-says-Meredith-suspect.html.

Morley, Sheridan (1992) 'Sharon's Stone-cold Touch', *Sunday Express*, 10 May, pp. 62–3.

Munn, Michael (1997) *The Sharon Stone Story*. London: Robson Books.

Nadeau, Barbie (2010) *Angel Face: The True Story of Student Killer Amanda Knox*. New York: Beast Books.

Nardi, Peter M. and Ralph Bolton (1998), 'Gay-bashing: Violence and Aggression against Gay Men and Lesbians', in Peter M. Nardi and Beth E. Schneider (eds), *Social Perspectives in Lesbian and Gay Studies: A Reader*. London and New York: Routledge.

Orlando Sentinel (1992) '"Instinct" Sizzles at Box Office', 24 March, accessed online 22 January 2012 at http://articles.orlandosentinel.com/1992-03-24/news/9203240046_ 1_queer-nation-basic-instinct-eszterhas.

O'Sullivan, Kevin (1992) 'Free Spirit under Fire – Michael Douglas', *Sunday Times*, 26 April.

Petley, Julian (2011) *Film and Video Censorship in Modern Britain*. Edinburgh: Edinburgh University Press.

Picardie, Ruth (1992) 'Mad, Bad and Dangerous', *New Statesman and Society* vol. 5 no. 200, 1 May, p. 36.

Pierce, Andrew (1995) 'Wife Stabbed Sailor after Watching *Basic Instinct*', *The Times*, 18 August, p. 3.

Pisa, Nick (2008) 'Foxy Knoxy Claims Female Cellmate Begs Her for Sex "Because I'm So Pretty"', *Mailonline*, 24 October, accessed online 12 January 2009 at http://www.dailymail. co.uk/news/worldnews/article-1080204/Foxy-Knoxy-claims-female-cell-mate-begs-sex-Im-pretty.html?ITO=1490.

Pisa, Nick (2011) 'Amanda Knox, the She-devil with a Dirty Soul: Lawyer's Tirade against Killer of Student Meredith Kercher', 27 September, accessed online 27 February 2012 at http://www.dailymail.co.uk/news/article-2041890/Amanda-Knox-murder-appeal-Lawyers-tirade-killer-Meredith-Kercher.html.

Pittsburgh Press (1992) '"Basic Instinct" Back as Box Office Leader', 28 April, p. C7.

Place, Janey (1980) 'Women in Film Noir', in E. Ann Kaplan (ed.), *Women in Film Noir*. London: BFI, pp. 35–67.

Popham, Peter (2009) 'Amanda Knox: Innocent Abroad, or a Calculating Killer? Now the Jury Must Decide', *Independent*, 16 January, accessed online 26 February 2012 at http://www.independent.co.uk/news/world/europe/ amanda-knox-innocent-abroad-or-a-calculating-killer-now-the-jury-must-decide-1380404.html.

Rafferty, Terrence (1992) 'Basic Instinct', *New Yorker*, 6 April, pp. 82–3.

Rohrer, Trish Dietch (1992) 'Adventures in the Skin Trade', *Entertainment Weekly*, 3 April, accessed online 14 December 2001 at http://www.ew.com/ew/article/0,,310048,00.html.

rottentomatoes.com (2009) 'Worst of the Worst', 23 September, accessed online 25 February 2012 at http://www.rottentomatoes.com/guides/ worst_of_the_worst/2/.

Rowbotham, Sheila (1997) *A Century of Women: The History of Women in Britain and the United States*. London: Viking Press.

Russo, Vito (1987) *The Celluloid Closet: Homosexuality in the Movies*. 2nd edn. London: HarperPaperbacks.

Sachs, Lloyd (1992) '"Basic Instinct" Debate: Removing the Element of Risk from the Movies', *Chicago Sun-Times*, 22 March, Show section, p. 1.

Sandler, Kevin S. (2007) *The Naked Truth: Why Hollywood Doesn't Make X-Rated Movies*. Rutgers, NJ and London: Rutgers University Press.

Sawtell, Jeff (1992) 'Basic Instinct', *Morning Star*, 9 May, p. 7.

van Scheers, Rob (1997) *Paul Verhoeven*, trans. Aletta Stevens. London: Faber and Faber.

Schickel, David (1992) 'Basic Instinct', *Time*, vol. 139 no. 12, 23 March, p. 65.

Sharrett, Christopher (1992) 'Hollywood Homophobia', *USA Today* vol. 120, July, p. 93.

Sheff, David (1992) Interview with Sharon Stone, *Playboy* magazine, December 1992, accessed online 1 October 2008 and reprinted at http://www.sharon-stone.eu/news/ 921200_mov_bi1_playboy.html.

Sherwin, Miranda (2008) 'Deconstructing the Male Gaze: Masochism, Female Spectatorship, and the Femme Fatale in *Fatal Attraction*, *Body of Evidence*, and *Basic Instinct*', *Journal of Popular Film and Television* vol. 35 no. 4, pp. 174–82.

Siegel, Carol (1995) 'Compulsory Heterophobia: The Aesthetics of Seriousness and the Production of Homophobia', in Carol Siegel and Ann Kibbey (eds), *Forming and Reforming Identity*. New York and London: New York University Press, pp. 319–38.

Silbey, Adrian (1990) 'The Loser Who Picked up Three Million Dollars', *Guardian*, 27 September, p. 25.

Simkin, Stevie (2005) *Early Modern Tragedy and the Cinema of Violence*. Basingstoke: Palgrave Macmillan.

Simpson, Janice C. (1992) 'Out of the Celluloid Closet: Gay Activists Are on a Rampage against Negative Stereotyping and Other Acts of Homophobia in Hollywood', *Time* vol. 139 no. 14, 6 April, p. 65.

Smeli, Anneke (2007) 'Lara Croft, *Kill Bill*, and the Battle for Theory in Feminist Film Studies', in Rosemarie Buikema and Iris van der Tuin (eds), *Doing Gender in Media, Art and Culture*. London and New York: Routledge.

Smith, Joan (1991) 'Film Forges Ahead Despite Gay Protest', *San Francisco Examiner*, 30 April, accessed 3 October 2008 online at http://www.toobeautiful.org/sfe0430.html.

Spicer, Andrew (2002) *Film Noir*. Harlow: Pearson Education Ltd.

Sun (1992) 22 April, from BBFC archive, cutting unpaginated.

Sun (2008), 'Knox Had "No Pants On in Jail"', 31 October, accessed online 12 January 2009 at http://www.thesun.co.uk/sol/homepage/news/article1873940.ece.

Sun Journal (2006) '"Ice Age" Snowballs with $70.5 Million, "Basic Instinct 2" Flops in Theaters', 3 April, p. B11.

Tasker, Yvonne (1993) *Spectacular Bodies: Gender, Genre and the Action Cinema*. London: Routledge.

Tasker, Yvonne (1994) 'Pussy Galore: Lesbian Images and Lesbian Desire in the Popular Cinema', in Diane Hamer and Belinda Budge (eds), *The Good, the Bad and the Gorgeous*. London: Pandora, pp. 172–83.

Time (1991) 'Censors on the Street', *Time* vol. 137 no. 19, 13 May, p. 70.

Tookey, Christopher (1992) 'Basic, but Good Dirty Fun', *Sunday Telegraph*, 10 May, p. III.

Tran, Mark (1992) 'Gays Cry Foul as Hollywood Picks a Bisexual Killer', *Guardian*, 18 March, p. 6.

Travers, Peter (1992) 'Basic Instinct', *Rolling Stone* no. 628, 20 March, accessed online 22 December 2011 at http://www.rollingstone.com/ movies/reviews/basic-instinct-19920320.

Turan, Kenneth (1992) 'Blood and Lust', *Los Angeles Times*, 20 March, p. F-1.

Usher, Peter (1992a) 'New "Last Tango" Upsets Censors', *Daily Mail*, 18 April.

Usher, Peter (1992b) 'Following the Instinct to Make a Fast Buck, Basically', *Daily Mail*, 8 May, p. 30.

Variety (1990) 'Ezsterhas Script Picks up Record $3-mil from Carolco', 27 June, pp. 10, 14.

Variety (1992) 'Basic Instinct', *Variety*, 1 January, accessed online 22 December 2011 at http://www.variety.com/index.asp?layout=review&reviewid=VE1117788888&categoryid=31&query=basic+instinct&display=basic+instinct&cs=1.

Vaughn, Stephen (2006) *Freedom and Entertainment: Rating the Movies in an Age of New Media*. Cambridge: Cambridge University Press.

Vindicator (1992) 'LA Riots Cut into Profits; "Instinct" Stays on Top', 5 May, p. B9.

Voynar, Kim (2006) 'Sharon Stone Gets in Touch with Those Kinky Instincts', *Cinematical*, 14 March, accessed online 25 February at http://blog.moviefone.com/2006/03/14/sharon-stone-gets-in-touch-with-those-kinky-instincts/.

Waites, Kate (2008) 'Babes in Boots: Hollywood's Oxymoronic Warrior Woman', in Suzanne Ferriss and Mallory Young (eds), *Chick Flicks: Contemporary Women at the Movies*. London: Routledge.

Walker, Alexander (1992) 'Trashy Thrills and Basic Instincts', *Evening Standard*, 7 May, p. 28.

Walker, Michael (1992) 'Film Noir: Introduction', in Ian Cameron (ed.), *The Movie Book of Film Noir*. London: Studio Vista/Cassell.

Weinraub, Bernard (1992) '"Basic Instinct": The Suspect Is Attractive, and May Be Fatal', *New York Times*, 15 March, accessed online 22 January 2012 at http://www.nytimes.com/1992/03/15/movies/film-basic-instinct-the-suspect-is-attractive-and-may-be-fatal.html.

Weir, John (1992) 'Gay-Bashing, Villainy and the Oscars', *New York Times*, 29 March, accessed online 17 February 2012 at http://www.nytimes.com/1992/03/29/movies/film-gay-bashing-villainy-and-the-oscars.html?pagewanted=all&src=pm.

Whatling, Clare (1997) *Screen Dreams: Fantasising Lesbians in Film*. Manchester and New York: Manchester University Press.

White, Diane (1992) 'This "Instinct" Isn't Basic, Just Base', *Boston Globe*, 25 March, p. 69.

Wilcox, Rhonda (2005) *Why Buffy Matters: The Art of Buffy the Vampire Slayer*. London: I. B. Tauris.

Wilcox, Rhonda and David Lavery (eds) (2002) *Fighting the Forces: What's at Stake in Buffy the Vampire Slayer*. London: Rowman & Littlefield Publishers.

Williams, Linda Ruth (2005) *The Erotic Thriller in Contemporary Cinema*. Edinburgh: Edinburgh University Press.

Williams, Linda Ruth (2006) 'Film of the Month: *Basic Instinct 2*', *Sight and Sound*, May, accessed online 25 February 2012 at http:// www.bfi.org.uk/sightandsound/review/3208.

Index

UNIVERSITY OF WINCHESTER
LIBRARY